REED ALEXANDER

KewlBites™

REED ALEXANDER

KewlBites™

100 Nutritious, Delicious, and Family-Friendly Dishes

© 2013 by Reed Alexander

Photographs © 2013 by Tara Donne

KewlBites™ is a trademark owned by KewlBites Inc.

Rodale books may be purchased for business or promotional use or for special sales.
For information, please write to:
Special Markets Department, Rodale, Inc., 733 Third Avenue, New York, NY 10017

Printed in the United States of America
Rodale Inc. makes every effort to use acid-free ♾, recycled paper ♲.

Book design by Amy C. King
Photography by Tara Donne
Food styling by Simon Andrews
Prop styling by Molly FitzSimons

Library of Congress Cataloging-in-Publication Data is on file with the publisher.
ISBN 978-1-60961-510-9   paperback

Distributed to the trade by Macmillan
2   4   6   8   10   9   7   5   3   1   paperback

We inspire and enable people to improve their lives and the world around them.
rodalebooks.com

For my amazing, inspiring mom

Contents

Introduction

WELCOME TO THE KEWLBITES™ KITCHEN, BY WAY OF MY VERY FIRST COOKBOOK! I'm so excited to share with you more than 100 delicious, healthy recipes that I know you and your family will love.

If you're looking for tasty, nutritious, and easy-to-make recipes, this book is for you. If you want to eat better and make smarter, more purposeful choices when selecting your ingredients, this book is for you. Whether you're a seasoned pro or just getting acquainted with your kitchen, this book is for you. And if you want your time in the kitchen to be super-fun, this book is definitely for you.

My desire to create **simple and healthful dishes** stems directly from my personal relationship with food. Up until a few years ago, my eating habits would have scored around a C+ on a nutrition report card. That was back when I didn't really realize the importance of eating healthfully and how a poor diet could affect my body. I thought "healthy" meant boring and dull. Needless to say, I was wrong!

Even though my eating habits weren't spot on (to be honest, far from it), I've always been a **major food lover!** I love to cook and create recipes, I'm a huge fan of cooking shows, and my family and I love discovering new restaurants. But it was only a few years ago that I realized that there was a connection between how I was eating and how I was feeling, which was not great. I was often tired, lacked confidence, and, overall, didn't feel my best. It took me some time to uncover the culprit, but gradually I began to make the connection between my out-of-control eating habits and my health. I needed to take matters into my own hands and **overhaul my lifestyle,** in particular the foods I was choosing.

After tons of research, I discovered that there were no solutions out there that were coming from a teen's point of view, no strategies that seemed to fit my life. So, I got to work in the kitchen and turned it into my laboratory, a place that I could experiment with my favorite (fattening) foods and make them healthier. I focused on the ingredients I was using, always looking for **more nutritious options** and healthier ways to infuse a dish with flavor. I ended up recreating my favorite comfort foods (and I bet they're yours, too) including pizza, meatballs, and apple pie. I was able to cut out some unhealthy elements and I discovered I could do this without sacrificing flavor and texture. It took some work—okay, a lot of work!—but I developed a huge array of recipes that passed muster with the most discerning audience of all—people just like me. Of course, my family was on the receiving end of many of my creations. I cooked most of these dishes for them and they loved the results! This made me want to share my **new cooking style** with more people and, of course, to end once and for all the lack of truly kid- and family-centric healthy recipes. As a result, I created my Web site, KewlBites.com, a super-fun, interactive online hub that allows me to connect with readers and visitors from all over the world. I never could have imagined the great response I received! I hadn't realized just how important this topic was for so many other people who were searching for ways to cook better for their families and build **healthy habits** early on.

So many amazing opportunities followed, from cooking live on national television shows—in both English and Spanish!—to developing **nutritious lunchtime recipes** and menus for thousands of schools across the country with President Clinton and the Clinton Foundation, to being invited to team up with First Lady Michelle Obama on her Let's Move! initiative, collaborating with the leaders of the USDA in Washington, DC, and more. Along the way, I've worked with extraordinary mentors, such as Food Network icons (and my big inspirations!) like Rachael Ray, Sunny Anderson, Melissa d'Arabian, and Ingrid Hoffmann. It has been an **incredible journey** that has truly enriched my life, as I hope it has for all of the people with whom I've been able to share my recipes, tips, and lessons learned, along with my KewlBites™ insight. And now, in the following pages I'm able to share all of that with you!

In this book, you're going to find recipes for every part of the day, and for nearly every occasion. All of the dishes have been fastidiously put to the test by me (and my hungry family members). I promise that they are **easy to make, delicious, and good for you.** Some of my personal favorites include Dark-Chocolate Banana Marble Bread (page 158), Mini Chicken Parm Meatballs (page 86), and Vegetable Dumplings with Lemongrass Dipping Sauce (page 139). My hope is that they'll be among yours, too. **Here's to healthy, happy cooking, and eating.**

BOCA RATON, FLORIDA
2013

1

Chapter ❶
Breakfast/Brunch

GOOD MORNING! The alarm clock has rung, you're suited up and ready to head out the door, most likely mulling over a to-do list that you intend to complete before you return home. But the task that sometimes is disregarded completely is the most important: breakfast. For many of us, it's the one meal that takes a backseat when it should be up front—because your body, like a car, is a machine that needs refueling at the start of each day.

In a perfect world, eating **a good breakfast** is a seamless step in the morning routine. But I know from experience that it can be a challenge, especially when it seems like every other obligation is far more important. With everything converging during those few morning minutes, who hasn't found themselves crushed by the chaos of completing everything on *yesterday's* list and worrying about what has to be taken care of today? In the fray, breakfast can easily become a casualty of the morning routine.

Many a morning has come and gone with my missing breakfast because of everything on my plate. It's normal! But I've learned that there's a happy medium between a mad dash and a multicourse morning meal. And it's where I like to hang out. So come and join me, and make a healthy breakfast part of your **daily routine**. Here are some ideas to help:

WEEKEND PREP. Even on busy weekends there's bound to be a block of time (think: an hour) available in your schedule for making and freezing breakfasts for the week ahead. Perfect example: You're sharing Sunday **brunch with your family,** enjoying a healthy helping of homemade Belgian Waffles (page 5). Why not whip up an extra batch? Wrap up two at a time in aluminum foil and freeze them. Come Monday morning, just unwrap a pack, microwave until warm (2 minutes usually does the trick), garnish with some fresh, sliced strawberries and a drizzle of pure maple syrup, and serve! It's an instant fiber-filled breakfast treat, minus the cardboard box. Or, try filling your freezer with my basic Classic Pancakes (page 7) or Orange French Toast (page 19).

TWENTY MINUTES ON THE CLOCK! I find 20 minutes to be a reasonable amount of time to sit down, take a deep breath, enjoy breakfast, and fit in a family powwow. Sometimes you'll have more or less time, but this tends to be enough.

SELF-STRATEGY SESSION. For me, breakfast is the first appointment of the day. You've had your restful night's sleep (I hope!), and you're ready to reenter the frenetic world. So why not pencil in an appointment with yourself? I'm a current events junkie, so I use breakfast as a time to watch the morning news, scan the headlines, and mentally sort through what's on tap for the day ahead. There's no reason you can't eat *and* work at the same time.

SCHEDULE SOLITAIRE. Develop a steady morning schedule for those hectic weekdays. Weekends can be free-style, but, from Monday through Friday, consistency is an important tool to use. Play around with your early morning agenda. Are you a shower-first/breakfast-later kind of person? Maybe you need to eat immediately after waking up and throwing off your covers. Whatever kind of morning person you are, find a method that works for you.

This is one tip that transcends breakfast and is all about personal preferences and setting yourself up for success throughout the day. No pressure here! There isn't a single right answer or ideal formula for finding the schedule that works for you. Feel free to try different ones until you discover a lineup that's most comfortable based on your needs and obligations. Go on—change it up! In no time, you'll have mastered the art of starting your mornings off right!

Belgian Waffles with Strawberry-Vanilla Glaze

YIELD: 8 to 10 medium-size square waffles

These powerhouse whole wheat waffles are crispy on the outside and as puffy as clouds on the inside. Belgian waffles have a naturally festive look and feel but are super-simple to whip up. I love to serve them on a Sunday morning for a fun family get-together; they're the ultimate crowd-pleaser! Drizzled with gooey Strawberry-Vanilla Glaze, they're delicious enough to satisfy any sweet tooth.

2 cups whole wheat flour

¼ cup raw sugar

1 tablespoon plus 1 teaspoon baking powder

⅛ teaspoon sea salt

1½ cups nonfat milk

½ cup unsweetened applesauce

4 large egg whites

2 teaspoons pure vanilla extract

Canola oil, for the waffle iron

Strawberry-Vanilla Glaze (page 6)

Follow the manufacturer's instructions to preheat a waffle iron to medium.

In a large mixing bowl, combine the flour, sugar, baking powder, and salt. In a separate bowl, combine the milk, applesauce, egg whites, and vanilla extract.

Pour the liquid mixture into the dry mixture and mix until just incorporated, with no lumps in the batter.

Lightly coat the waffle iron with oil. Working in batches if necessary, pour the appropriate amount of batter into the wells of the waffle iron, close the lid, and bake until golden brown (per manufacturer's instructions).

Remove the waffles to a serving dish. Serve with (or topped by) the Strawberry-Vanilla Glaze.

Strawberry-Vanilla Glaze

YIELD: Approximately 3 cups

Use this flavorful glaze to top off waffles instead of overdoing it with all that excessive maple syrup. Or eat it on its own by the spoonful—a satisfying, stand-alone treat!

2 vanilla beans

1 quart strawberries, cut into ½-inch-thick slices

1½ cups brewed decaffeinated vanilla-flavored tea (steeped in hot water), tea leaves discarded

¾ cup freshly squeezed orange juice

¼ cup light agave nectar

½ teaspoon pure vanilla extract

Slice the vanilla beans in half lengthwise and scrape out the seeds. Reserve both scraped seeds and bean pods.

In a large, wide sauté pan with high sides, combine the vanilla seeds and pods, the strawberries, tea, orange juice, and agave nectar. Simmer over medium heat, stirring occasionally, until the mixture is substantially reduced and the strawberries are tender, resulting in a thick, syrupy compote, 45 to 50 minutes.

Stir in the vanilla extract and cook 1 to 2 minutes more. Discard the vanilla pods. Set aside to cool for approximately 5 minutes.

Serve alongside (or atop) waffles, warm or chilled.

Classic Pancakes

YIELD: **10 pancakes**

Transport the flavors of your local pancake house straight to your breakfast table with this light, homemade version of the classic morning favorite. Made with egg whites, nonfat milk, and a combination of flours, these tender pancakes are the perfect balance of texture and fluff. The fiber-rich mix is easy to whip up for breakfast or brunch, and it's even easier to keep the cooked pancakes, wrapped tightly in aluminum foil, on hand in the freezer. Warm them at a low temperature in the oven when you need a quick fix on a busy morning.

1 cup all-purpose flour

½ cup whole wheat flour

1 tablespoon raw sugar

1 teaspoon baking powder

1 teaspoon baking soda

¼ teaspoon sea salt

1 cup nonfat milk

1 large egg, lightly beaten

2 large egg whites, lightly beaten

2 tablespoons canola oil, plus extra for coating the pan

In a large bowl, combine the all-purpose and whole wheat flours, sugar, baking powder, baking soda, and salt. In a separate bowl, combine the milk, egg, egg whites, and oil. Pour the liquid mixture into the dry mixture and gently combine just until no lumps remain, being careful not to overmix.

Heat a nonstick skillet over medium heat and lightly coat with canola oil. Ladle about ¼ cup batter for each pancake into the pan,* being sure not to crowd the pan. Cook until bubbles begin to form in the center, 4 to 5 minutes. Flip** and cook 3 minutes more, until done. Repeat with remaining batter.

*TIP: To prevent the batter from running when you spoon it onto the griddle, make sure your pan is hot.

**TIP: Limit the number of times you flip each pancake to just ONCE! When bubbles appear and the edges are browned, flip! More than one flip could cause the pancakes to overcook and become tough.

Cherry-Currant Scones

YIELD: 10 to 12 scones

These fruit-studded treats are inspired by my visits to London. It's one of my favorite cities and the place I love to indulge in afternoon tea, complete with authentic scones. With ingredients like heart-healthy canola oil and unsweetened applesauce, they don't need butter and are so much lighter than their traditional counterparts. Instead of opting for clotted cream, spread a spoonful of glistening jam, jelly, or marmalade on the scones when they're warm from the oven.

1½ cups self-rising flour

½ cup whole wheat pastry flour

1 teaspoon baking powder

¼ teaspoon sea salt

½ cup nonfat milk

¼ cup canola oil

¼ cup unsweetened applesauce

1 teaspoon freshly grated orange zest

⅓ cup dried cherries, coarsely chopped

⅓ cup dried currants, coarsely chopped

1 large egg

1 teaspoon water

Preheat the oven to 400°F. Line a large baking sheet with parchment paper.

In a mixing bowl, combine the self-rising and whole wheat flours, baking powder, and salt. In a separate bowl, combine the milk, oil, applesauce, and orange zest.

Pour the liquid mixture into the dry and mix until just combined. Stir in the cherries and currants.

Scoop 2 tablespoons of the dough, roll into a ball, place on the sheet, and press down slightly to flatten. Scoop 2 more tablespoons of dough, roll into a ball, set on top of the flattened dough, and press down to likewise flatten and form a double-layered scone. Repeat with the remaining batter to make 10 to 12 scones, placing them 2 inches apart on the sheet.

Lightly beat the egg with the water. Lightly brush the tops and edges of the scones with the egg wash using a pastry brush.

Bake for 16 to 18 minutes, or until the scones are puffed and golden brown. Serve warm.

Blueberry-Pomegranate Yogurt Parfaits

YIELD: 4 parfaits

These parfaits are the spot-on solution for on-the-run mornings, provided you follow my lead and always have a container of blueberry-pomegranate syrup stashed in the fridge. The combination of tart pomegranate juice, warm vanilla, and crunchy granola is an unbeatable mix. Some of the plusses: Blueberries + pomegranate = a bounty of antioxidants; yogurt is a fantastic source of filling protein and calcium; and this recipe is all-around delicious, fast, and easy!

2 cups unsweetened pomegranate juice

3 tablespoons raw sugar

1½ cups frozen blueberries

1 teaspoon pure vanilla extract

2 cups nonfat vanilla yogurt, organic if you can find it

4 tablespoons granola

In a saucepan, bring the pomegranate juice and sugar to a boil over medium-high heat. Simmer, uncovered, until thick enough to coat the back of a spoon, 7 to 8 minutes.

Add the blueberries, reduce the heat to medium low, and simmer, stirring occasionally, until the blueberries soften, 10 minutes.

Stir in the vanilla extract and simmer 15 minutes more, until the blueberries are tender. Remove from the heat. If desired, chill the syrup in the refrigerator for 1 hour or until cold.

To assemble the parfaits, place ½ cup yogurt into each of 4 parfait glasses. Top each with 3 to 4 tablespoons of the blueberry-pomegranate syrup, sprinkle with 1 tablespoon granola, and enjoy!

Breakfast Pizza

YIELD: 6 servings

The toppings on these crustless egg wedges are the secret to their fantastic flavor: Caramelized shallots provide sweetness while the robust, chewy mushrooms and fresh sautéed spinach round out each hearty bite. I've specified easy-to-find button mushrooms for this recipe, but you can be adventurous: Cremini, oyster, portobello, and shiitake are all great alternatives.

1 tablespoon olive oil

2 medium shallots, thinly sliced into rounds

2¼ cups thinly sliced button mushrooms

2 cups spinach leaves

½ cup minced fresh chives or scallions, plus extra to garnish

3 large eggs

4 large egg whites

3 tablespoons nonfat milk

⅛ teaspoon sea salt

⅛ teaspoon ground black pepper

½ cup shredded reduced-fat American cheese

Heat the oil in a large nonstick skillet over medium heat. Once the oil begins to shimmer, add the shallots and sauté until softened, 3 to 4 minutes.

Add the mushrooms and cook until the juices are released and have begun to reduce, 5 to 7 minutes. Add the spinach and cook until slightly wilted, 1 to 2 minutes. Fold in the chives and cook 1 minute to warm through. Remove from the heat.

In a small bowl, whisk together the eggs, egg whites, milk, salt, and pepper.

Using a paper towel, wipe out the skillet, then set over medium-low heat. Pour in half of the egg mixture and cook until the bottom has just set, 4 to 5 minutes. Using a spatula, push the cooked egg from the edges to the center while tipping the pan, allowing any uncooked egg to run onto the hot surface.* Once all the egg is set, transfer to a serving plate and set aside. Repeat with the remaining egg mixture.

To assemble, top each egg pizza with half of the mushroom filling, spreading it evenly. Sprinkle with the cheese and garnish with chives. Cut each pizza into 6 wedges.

When cooking the eggs, the idea is to create an open-faced omelet rather than the traditional folded style. Use a nonstick silicone spatula to make the process of pushing the cooked egg inward just a little bit easier. (My nonstick spatula is one of my culinary BFFs—I use it time and time again. If you don't have one, get one; it's a great, cost-effective item to invest in.)

Margherita Frittata

YIELD: 6 servings

Do you know the history of *Pizza Margherita,* the famous concoction from the local trattoria that's made of creamy white mozzarella, emerald green basil, and ruby red tomatoes? It was invented for Her Majesty Queen Margherita of Savoy, the queen consort of Italy who lived in the late 19th and early 20th centuries. I've taken those three ingredients from the classic pizza and mixed them into an open-faced omelet for a delicious breakfast. Made in a skillet, it moves seamlessly from stovetop to oven to table. Slice it into wedges like a traditional pizza and serve with a simple green salad on the side—for breakfast, lunch, or dinner.

5 large eggs

5 large egg whites

¼ cup nonfat milk

3 tablespoons thinly sliced basil, divided

¼ teaspoon sea salt

Ground black pepper, to taste

2 roma tomatoes, sliced into ½-inch rounds

3 ounces fresh mozzarella cheese, cut into ½-inch cubes or triangles

Preheat the oven to 350°F. Lightly coat a 10-inch nonstick ovenproof skillet with olive oil and set over medium-high heat.

In a mixing bowl, whisk together the eggs, egg whites, milk, 2 tablespoons of the basil, the salt, and pepper. Once the skillet is hot, reduce the heat to medium low and add the egg mixture. Cook, occasionally running a heatproof spatula around the edge of the skillet to push the cooked egg into the liquid mixture and allow raw egg to run underneath, until the mixture is mostly set but still liquid on the surface and in the center, 5 to 6 minutes.

Carefully arrange the tomato slices on top and then evenly sprinkle with the cheese and the remaining 1 tablespoon basil. If necessary, gently push the ingredients into the surface of the liquid egg with the spatula. Transfer the skillet to the oven and bake for 2 to 3 minutes, until the frittata is golden and slightly puffed.

Allow the frittata to rest in the pan for 2 to 3 minutes, and then carefully slide it out onto a heatproof serving dish. Cut into 6 wedges and serve.

Dill-Feta Egg White Pockets

YIELD: 6 pockets

Using only egg whites helps to cut back on unnecessary fat and cholesterol in these flavorful, colorful pocket sandwiches. They're so filling that you'll never miss the egg yolks. This recipe cracks the code on the most delicious and good-for-you breakfast sandwich around!

3 (6-inch) whole wheat pitas, halved crosswise

12 large egg whites

¼ cup nonfat milk

3 tablespoons olive oil

¼ cup diced yellow onion

1 medium yellow bell pepper, cored, seeded, and cut into thin strips

1 medium red bell pepper, cored, seeded, and cut into thin strips

¼ teaspoon sea salt

¼ teaspoon ground black pepper

¼ cup crumbled feta cheese

¼ cup coarsely chopped fresh dill, plus extra for garnish

Preheat the oven to 350°F. Cover a baking sheet with aluminum foil. Place the pita pockets on the sheet and bake for 3 to 5 minutes, until lightly toasted. Cover with aluminum foil to keep warm and set aside.

In a medium bowl, whisk together the egg whites and milk. Set aside.

Heat the oil in a large sauté pan or skillet over medium heat. Add the onions and bell peppers, season with salt and pepper, and sauté until tender, about 10 minutes.

Pour the egg white mixture into the pan and, using a heatproof spatula, gently push the whites back and forth until they begin to break apart. Continue scrambling until the eggs are loose but no longer in a liquid state, 3 to 4 minutes. Fold in the feta cheese and scramble until there is no liquid left and the egg whites are fully cooked, about 4 minutes more. Fold in the fresh dill.

To assemble the pita pockets, evenly divide the egg mixture among the 6 toasted pocket halves, being careful not to tear the pockets. Garnish with extra dill.

Steel-Cut Apple-Pie Oatmeal

YIELD: 4 servings

Make a stovetop version of rich, flavorful apple pie filling starring warm spices like cinnamon and cardamom. Generously mound it on top of homemade steel-cut oats. Then indulge in a delicious, fiber-filled breakfast.

¼ cup freshly squeezed orange juice

¼ cup water

3 tablespoons honey

1 teaspoon ground cinnamon

½ teaspoon ground cardamom

⅛ teaspoon sea salt

2 large Fuji apples, peeled, cored, and chopped into ½-inch chunks

¼ cup raisins

1 teaspoon pure vanilla extract

4 cups water

1 cup steel-cut oats

Coarsely chopped walnuts (optional)

In a large sauté pan, bring the orange juice, the ¼ cup water, honey, cinnamon, cardamom, and salt to a simmer over medium heat. Reduce to medium low, add the apples, and cook, stirring occasionally, until the apples are tender and the liquid has reduced to a thick syrup, 20 to 25 minutes. Stir in the raisins and vanilla extract and cook 2 to 3 minutes more. Remove from the heat.

Meanwhile, combine the 4 cups water and the oats in a medium saucepan and gently simmer over medium-low heat until the oats are tender and water is absorbed, 30 to 35 minutes.

Divide the oatmeal evenly among 4 serving bowls. Top each with one-fourth of the apple-raisin mixture. Sprinkle with walnuts, if desired.

Orange French Toast

Kick off the morning with a little vitamin C and flavors like sweet vanilla, warm cinnamon, and yummy allspice! This nutritious take on French toast is easy, delicious, and really satisfying—a high-octane breakfast that is sure to keep you going until lunchtime. I concede that this breakfast treat probably won't whisk you off to Paris, but you're guaranteed a great start to an amazing day!

6 large egg whites

1 tablespoon nonfat milk

1 teaspoon grated orange zest

½ teaspoon pure vanilla extract

⅛ teaspoon ground cinnamon

⅛ teaspoon ground allspice

4 slices 100 percent whole grain bread

1 orange, peeled and sliced

4 teaspoons pure maple syrup, for serving

Lightly coat a large nonstick skillet with canola oil and set over medium-high heat.

In a shallow bowl, whisk together the egg whites, milk, orange zest, vanilla extract, cinnamon, and allspice and mix well. Dip each slice of bread into the egg white mixture to coat on both sides.

Place the bread slices in the pan and cook 2 to 4 minutes per side, or until golden brown.

Place 2 slices of French toast on each of 2 serving plates. Top each slice with orange slices and 1 teaspoon syrup and serve.

Cherries Jubilee Quinoa

YIELD: 4 servings

Cherries Jubilee for breakfast? The first meal of the day just became a whole lot sweeter. And, when you combine it with quinoa, a whole lot healthier as well. Quinoa, one of the greatest sources of protein outside of meat, poultry, or fish, cooks up just like rice and has the same fluffy texture. This breakfast version is fragrant with cinnamon and vanilla and studded with sweet dates and fresh cherries.

- 1 cup whole grain quinoa, rinsed
- 2 cups unsweetened almond milk
- 1½ cups fresh cherries, stems removed, sliced in half, and pitted
- ½ cup coarsely chopped dried dates, plus extra for garnish

- 1½ tablespoons raw sugar
- 1½ teaspoons ground cinnamon
- 1½ teaspoons pure vanilla extract
- ⅛ teaspoon sea salt

In a medium saucepan over medium heat, combine the quinoa and milk. Cover and simmer until the quinoa is al dente and has absorbed all of the milk, 12 to 15 minutes. (If using packaged—as opposed to bulk—quinoa, follow the package instructions to prepare.)

Remove the pan from the heat and stir in the cherries, dates, sugar, cinnamon, vanilla extract, and salt. Mix well until completely combined. Divide the mixture evenly among 4 bowls, garnish with dates, and serve.

Power Fusion Breakfast Blend

YIELD: 2 servings

This recipe's name says it all. Inspired by the tropical flavors of the Caribbean, it's one of my favorite ways to kick-start the day. This smoothie is a nutrition powerhouse—mangoes provide iron, flaxseeds furnish the fiber, ginger soothes the stomach, and coconut water offers essential hydration with electrolytes and potassium (both important for preventing muscle cramps after a workout). I always blend up a batch after exercising.

2 tablespoons flaxseeds

¾ cup frozen unsweetened mango chunks

¾ cup frozen unsweetened pineapple chunks

1 medium kiwi, peeled and quartered

2 teaspoons coarsely chopped fresh ginger

½ cup freshly squeezed orange juice

½ cup coconut water

2 tablespoons light agave nectar

1 teaspoon coconut extract

Pulse the flaxseeds in a blender on high speed until crushed into a fine powder.

Add the mango, pineapple, kiwi, ginger, orange juice, coconut water, agave nectar, and coconut extract to the blender and puree on high speed until completely smooth, 1 to 2 minutes. Pour into 2 serving glasses and serve.

Triple-Berry Blend

YIELD: 2 servings

I use frozen berries as opposed to fresh because, nutritionally, they're equivalent and just as beneficial. The big difference: Frozen fruits are like mini ice pops. When you blend them into a smoothie, the resulting texture will be creamy and super-luscious. Almond milk is a fantastic nondairy way to go, but feel free to use nonfat milk or another option you prefer.

¾ cup frozen unsweetened blueberries

¾ cup frozen unsweetened strawberries

¾ cup frozen unsweetened raspberries

1 cup unsweetened plain almond milk

⅓ cup nonfat plain yogurt

2 tablespoons light agave nectar

2 teaspoons pure vanilla extract

In a blender, puree the blueberries, strawberries, raspberries, milk, yogurt, agave nectar, and vanilla extract until completely smooth, 1½ to 2 minutes.

Pour the smoothie into 2 serving glasses. Enjoy!

Chapter ❷
Soups/Salads/Sandwiches

PACKING A HEALTHY SALAD, SANDWICH, OR SOUP INTO YOUR DAILY ROUTINE CAN BE THE PERFECT WAY TO INCORPORATE HEARTY, NOURISHING VEGETABLES, GRAINS, AND PROTEIN INTO YOUR DIET. Now, for a personal confession: I used to steer clear of the dreaded iceberg lettuce (and, as a result, any salad at all), convinced that its pale, flavorless leaves were the only option out there when it came to greens. But, after putting some thought into my quest for better salads, I discovered that the produce section and farmers' markets are loaded with vibrant varieties of different greens, such as red leaf, arugula, and romaine—and every one is way more nutritious (and tastier) than iceberg!

I'm so excited to share my **seasonal salads** in the following pages, each one designed around the fresh produce and flavors of winter, spring, summer, and fall. Use them as blueprints, and tailor them to your own liking. The key is to incorporate a balance of ingredients, with the greens taking **center stage.** An excess of cheese, nuts, or creamy dressings can be the surefire way to weigh down the nutritious, delicious satisfaction of a fresh salad—one that you'll want to eat. A couple of kewl tips will help to keep your salad from veering off in the wrong direction:

SALAD DRESSING: When it comes to salad dressing, think OTS. . . . that is, On The Side. This will be dressing's new home, forevermore. Instead of pouring it all over the greens, dip your fork into it before you take each bite. This way, you'll master **portion control** and avoid falling into the trap of drenching your greens in fat, oil, and sometimes sugar or artificial preservatives.

NUTS AND CHEESES: Think of both of these ingredients as accessories, not main ingredients. Using them with a light hand adds exponential flavor to your salad, but a heavy hand will do just the opposite—it weighs it down and overwhelms all the good stuff.

In addition to superstar salads, you'll also find recipes for hearty sandwiches and soups in this chapter. While most of these are great for lunch, they're also perfect to plate up for dinner. The great thing about soup is that it requires only one pot, is forgiving when it comes to cooking, and is an amazing vehicle for protein, fiber-rich grains, and nutritious vegetables. What's more, you can make extra and enjoy it the next day or freeze it for those times when cooking isn't in the cards. Here are some tips:

JUST A FEW GRAINS OF SALT. Season soups with salt sparingly and avoid adding salt directly to the broth or liquid while it's cooking. This enables each of your guests to sprinkle a dash in at the table and use it according to their own taste, thereby reducing sodium—an ingredient that lurks in almost everything we eat.

USE LOW-SODIUM CHICKEN BROTH AND BEANS. Broth is fundamental to any soup. Take the opportunity to cut back on salt by using low-sodium store-bought chicken, beef, vegetable, and seafood broth. The same goes for beans. (Of course, fresh is best—but I'm a realist!)

Sandwiches are universally enjoyed by everyone and, with a little know-how on your side, you can upgrade the traditional turkey-on-rye or basic peanut butter-and-jelly standards and create your own super-nutritious combination. The best part? Your homemade sandwich is easily portable and on hand to take to work, school, the beach, or a weekend picnic. In this chapter, you'll find the good old standbys, including egg and tuna salads, lightened up and reinvigorated with fresh herbs, nuts, and fruits, eliminating the need for heavy condiments like mayonnaise or ketchup for flavor. And with just a few tips in your back pocket, you can make delicious sandwiches that are good for you, too:

SKIP WHITE FOR WHEAT. The less wheat is processed, the better it is for you. If you can buy your bread from a local baker, go for it. Whole wheat beats white, and if the ingredient list stops after or contains little more than whole wheat flour, yeast, water, and salt, you can feel even better. Not only is whole wheat healthier, but it tastes so much nuttier and has a more satisfying, fuller flavor.

KEEP AN OPEN FACE. I love open-faced sandwiches; by eating half as much bread, you can cut down on unnecessary carbohydrates while simultaneously enjoying a better view of all of the colorful ingredients inside.

Multigrain Chicken Soup

YIELD: **8 servings**

A staple in my fridge or freezer, this chicken soup is a one-pot wonder, chock-full of fresh herbs, hearty vegetables, and juicy chicken. In lieu of noodles, I use a mixture of whole grain basmati rice and wild rice. Considered a cure-all for the common cold, chicken soup will also replenish your strength and revitalize your energy—it's a warm, embracing elixir to melt away the chill. Try this once and trust me, it will become part of your family's cool-weather repertoire.

1 leek, halved and thoroughly washed

7 sprigs fresh flat-leaf parsley

7 sprigs fresh dill

4 sprigs fresh thyme

2 sprigs fresh rosemary

2 fresh bay leaves

1½ tablespoons olive oil

1½ sweet yellow onions, diced

2 cloves garlic, minced

1 whole chicken (about 4½ pounds)

6 cups low-sodium chicken broth

12 cups water, divided

⅔ cup whole grain brown basmati rice

⅔ cup wild rice

4 medium carrots, diced

4 large stalks celery, diced

2 medium parsnips, diced

½ medium rutabaga, diced

Dice the white and light green parts of the leek and set aside. Tie the rigid dark green parts together with kitchen string. Gather the parsley, dill, thyme, rosemary, and bay leaves into a bunch and tie with kitchen twine. Set both bunches aside.

Heat the oil in a large 7-quart saucepan or Dutch oven over medium-high heat. When it begins to shimmer, add the onions and garlic. Cook, stirring occasionally, until browned and very fragrant, 15 to 20 minutes.

Carefully place the chicken into the pan and add the broth, 6 cups of the water, and the bundles of herbs and leek tops. Cover, raise the heat to high, and bring to a boil (which may take up to 20 to 30 minutes). *Reduce the heat and simmer until the chicken has cooked through (when a leg is wiggled it should easily pull away from the joint), about 1 hour.

Meanwhile, after 30 minutes, combine the basmati rice, wild rice, and remaining 6 cups water in a saucepan. Set over high heat, stir, and bring to a boil. Reduce the heat, cover, and simmer until the rice is tender and the water is absorbed, about 30 minutes. Lightly fluff with a fork and transfer to a heatproof dish. Cover with aluminum foil and set aside.

When the chicken is cooked, carefully transfer it to a plate and let cool 5 minutes. Remove the herb and leek bundles. If desired, remove the twine, coarsely chop the herbs and leek tops, and return to the soup.

Stir the diced white and light green parts of the leek, the carrots, celery, parsnips, and rutabaga into the soup. Cover and cook over high heat until tender, 15 minutes. Remove the soup from the heat.

When the chicken is cool enough to be handled safely, discard the skin and remove the meat from the bones. Shred the meat into bite-size chunks by pulling it apart with a fork. Return the meat to the soup and stir to combine.

Divide the rice among 8 soup bowls and ladle generous helpings of soup over each serving. Season with salt and pepper to taste.

*TIP: Boiling leek tops infuses the broth with potent flavors and tenderizes them to the point where they melt in your mouth. "Steeping" the herbs in the liquid is another way to impart strong flavor to the broth.

Asian Shrimp-Udon Soup

YIELD: **5 servings**

Plump shrimp, spicy fresh ginger, bright lemongrass, an array of veggies, and whole wheat udon noodles, a staple in the Japanese pantry, are showcased in this intoxicating Asian soup. If you can't find them, use 8 ounces of whole wheat spaghetti instead.

2 tablespoons canola oil, divided

¾ pound raw shrimp, peeled and deveined

¾ teaspoon sea salt, divided

½ teaspoon ground black pepper

3 medium shallots, sliced into thin rounds

2 stalks lemongrass, tops, bottoms, and outer layers of stalks discarded, stalks sliced in half and smashed with the side of a knife

1 tablespoon minced fresh ginger

2 teaspoons light brown sugar

5½ cups low-sodium vegetable broth

3½ ounces shiitake mushrooms, stems removed and quartered

1 (4-ounce) can water chestnuts, drained

½ cup bean sprouts

1 medium head bok choy, sliced

1 (8-ounce) package 100 percent whole wheat udon noodles

1 tablespoon reduced-sodium soy sauce

8 large fresh basil leaves, torn

2 medium scallions, sliced into rounds, for garnish (optional)

½ cup shredded carrots, for garnish (optional)

½ cup fresh cilantro leaves, for garnish (optional)

Heat 1 tablespoon of the oil in a large saucepan or Dutch oven over medium-high heat. When the oil is very hot, carefully add the shrimp and stir. Season with ½ teaspoon of the salt and the pepper. Sauté until almost cooked through (the shrimp will finish cooking later). Remove to a dish and set aside.

(continued)

Add the remaining 1 tablespoon oil to the pan. Add the shallots and season with the remaining ¼ teaspoon salt. Reduce the heat to medium and sauté until the shallots are tender, about 2 minutes. Add the lemongrass, ginger, and brown sugar and cook, stirring, until very fragrant, about 1 minute.

Add the vegetable broth, scraping the bottom of the pan to release the flavorful brown bits. Raise the heat to medium high and cook just until the soup boils, and then reduce to a simmer. Add the mushrooms, water chestnuts, bean sprouts, and bok choy. Cook, stirring occasionally, until the vegetables are tender, 5 to 7 minutes.

Meanwhile, bring a separate pot of water to a boil over high heat. Add the udon noodles and cook according to package instructions until al dente. Drain.

Add the shrimp and udon noodles to the soup and cook until the noodles are completely tender and the shrimp are cooked through, 2 to 3 minutes. Discard the lemongrass stalks and stir in the soy sauce and basil.

Divide the noodles and shrimp among 5 soup bowls. Ladle the broth over them and garnish with scallions, carrots, and cilantro, if using.

Grilled Summer Vegetable Salad with Balsamic Vinaigrette

YIELD: **4 servings**

This salad is a surefire signal that summer has officially arrived. From charred corn, juicy tomatoes, and tender squash and zucchini to vivid green sprigs of fresh dill, it captures the essence of the season in every single bite.

FOR THE SALAD

4 medium yellow squash, halved lengthwise

3 medium zucchini, halved lengthwise

2 large ears corn, husks removed

¾ pound asparagus spears, tough white stems removed

1 avocado, cut into ½-inch cubes

¾ cup red grape tomatoes, halved

¾ cup yellow grape tomatoes, halved

3 cups mixed greens

¼ cup coarsely chopped fresh dill

FOR THE BALSAMIC VINAIGRETTE

½ cup olive oil

2 tablespoons balsamic vinegar

1 tablespoon Dijon mustard

1 clove garlic, peeled

2 teaspoons dried basil

Preheat the grill to high or heat a grill pan over high heat on the stovetop. Lightly brush the squash, zucchini, corn, and asparagus with olive oil and season with salt and pepper on all sides. Grill the squash and zucchini, cut sides down, for 8 to 10 minutes. Flip and grill for 4 to 5 minutes more. Grill the corn, turning every 5 minutes, until browned and lightly charred, 25 to 30 minutes. Grill the asparagus until charred, turning once, 6 to 8 minutes. Or, place the asparagus on a baking sheet lined with aluminum foil and roast in an oven set at a temperature of 400°F for 10 minutes. Let the vegetables cool for 5 to 10 minutes. Slice the squash, zucchini, and asparagus into ½-inch chunks. Slice the corn from the cobs. Transfer to a large mixing bowl and gently toss with the avocado, tomatoes, greens, and dill. Season with salt and pepper to taste.

Combine the oil, vinegar, mustard, garlic, and basil in a blender or food processor. Pulse until smooth. Season with salt and pepper. Drizzle over the salad and toss to coat.

Golden Nugget Winter Salad

YIELD: **4 servings**

Coming up with salads during the cold months can sometimes be a challenge. This winter, warm up your appetite with the delicious flavors of roasted golden beets, sunny oranges, and toasted maple pecans. Topped with feta cheese and a light raspberry vinaigrette, this hearty, nutritious salad is one of my wintertime favorites.

4 golden beets, skins on, stems removed

1 cup unsalted raw pecans

¼ cup pure Grade A maple syrup

2 tablespoons plus 2 teaspoons olive oil

1 tablespoon plus 1 teaspoon raspberry vinegar

4 cups mixed greens or spinach leaves

1 orange, peeled and separated into segments

½ cup crumbled feta cheese

Preheat the oven to 425°F. Wrap the beets tightly in aluminum foil. Place on a baking sheet and bake for 60 to 70 minutes, until just fork-tender. Set aside to cool.

Line the baking sheet with aluminum foil and coat lightly with canola oil. Toss the pecans with the maple syrup on the sheet. Reduce the oven temperature to 350°F. Bake the pecans, stirring after 10 minutes and being cautious to prevent burning, for about 15 minutes, until toasted. Set aside to cool.

Meanwhile, make the dressing: Combine the olive oil, vinegar, and salt and pepper to taste in a small bowl and set aside.

When the beets have cooled, slice off the tops and bottoms and peel with your hands or a knife. Discard the skins. Slice each beet into 7 or 8 thin rounds.

To assemble the salads, arrange 1 cup of greens or spinach on each of 4 plates. Arrange 7 or 8 beet slices (1 total beet) on top of each salad. Divide the orange segments evenly among the plates, followed by the toasted nuts and 2 tablespoons feta cheese. Serve with the dressing on the side.

Autumn Arugula Salad with Pomegranate Dressing

YIELD: **4 servings**

The fall harvest has arrived! Toss golden roasted butternut squash, tart pomegranate seeds, sweet dried cranberries, and crunchy toasted pumpkin seeds with fresh mixed greens, then drizzle with a burgundy pomegranate dressing for the ultimate seasonal salad.

FOR THE POMEGRANATE DRESSING

1 cup unsweetened pomegranate juice

¼ cup olive oil

1 tablespoon honey

1 teaspoon champagne vinegar

1½ teaspoons grated orange zest

FOR THE SALAD

1 (1½-pound) butternut squash, peeled, seeded, and cut into ½-inch cubes

2 tablespoons minced fresh sage

2 tablespoons olive oil

½ teaspoon sea salt

½ teaspoon ground black pepper

3 cups arugula or mixed greens

½ cup pumpkin or squash seeds, toasted*

½ cup dried cranberries

½ cup pomegranate seeds

½ cup crumbled goat cheese

To make the dressing, simmer the pomegranate juice, uncovered, in a saucepan over medium-high heat until reduced by half, about 15 minutes. Chill in the refrigerator until cold. Combine the chilled, reduced pomegranate juice with the olive oil, honey, vinegar, and orange zest in a food processor and process until blended. Season with salt and pepper.

To make the salad, preheat the oven to 375°F. On a baking sheet lined with aluminum foil, toss the squash with the sage, oil, salt, and pepper. Roast, stirring halfway through, for 35 to 40 minutes, or until tender.

In a large bowl, toss together the arugula or greens, pumpkin or squash seeds, cranberries, and pomegranate seeds. Add the squash and gently toss to combine. Divide among 4 serving dishes. Drizzle each with 2 to 3 tablespoons dressing (or to taste) or serve it on the side. Top each salad with 2 tablespoons cheese.

TIP: Toasting nuts or seeds is super-simple! It unlocks the deep, nutty flavors of any nut or seed within a matter of minutes. For this salad, spread dry, raw pumpkin seeds on an ungreased baking sheet lined with aluminum foil, then toast in a 325°F oven for 20 to 30 minutes, stirring occasionally. You'll notice their fragrance beginning to permeate your kitchen, and the seeds will turn golden. Toss them into the salad here or into trail mix, or enjoy a handful on their own, sprinkled with a little sea salt. Pumpkin seeds are rich in key nutrients like zinc, which fortifies your immune system, and magnesium, which contributes to strong bones and teeth.

P³ Spring Salad with Green Goddess Dressing

YIELD: **4 servings**

Spring has sprung with a variety of "P" ingredients! "P-cubed" means crunchy English **peas,** bright Italian **parsley,** and freshly grated **Parmesan**. Add diced cucumbers and a creamy Green Goddess dressing, and this simple salad brims with garden-fresh looks and flavors.

FOR THE GREEN GODDESS DRESSING

¾ cup low-fat mayonnaise

¾ cup light sour cream

½ cup coarsely chopped scallions, both white and green parts

¼ cup lemon juice

1 tablespoon Worcestershire sauce

2 teaspoons minced fresh chives

2 cloves garlic, peeled

½ teaspoon sea salt

¼ teaspoon ground black pepper

FOR THE SALAD

1 cup English peas

½ medium English cucumber, seeded and diced

¼ cup minced fresh flat-leaf parsley

8 large Boston Bibb lettuce leaves

½ cup grated Parmesan cheese

To make the dressing, combine the mayonnaise, sour cream, scallions, lemon juice, Worcestershire sauce, chives, garlic, salt, and pepper in a blender. Pulse until the mixture is smooth and completely combined. Transfer to the refrigerator and chill at least 1 hour before serving.

To make the salad, bring a medium saucepan of water to a boil over high heat. Add the peas and blanch for 1 minute. Drain and cool.

In a large mixing bowl, combine the peas, cucumber, and parsley. Add about 1 cup chilled dressing (or to taste) and mix to combine.

On each of 4 serving plates, layer 2 overlapping lettuce leaves. Divide the dressed salad evenly among the 4 plates, piling it in the center of the leaves. Garnish each with 2 tablespoons Parmesan and serve.

Tricolor Caesar Salad with Whole Grain Rosemary Croutons

YIELD: **4 servings**

I've shaken up the classic Caesar salad with a kewl twist! I've added frisée and red leaf lettuce to romaine both to give a visual boost and to vary the texture of this delicious salad. With homemade Whole Grain Rosemary Croutons and a lightened-up Caesar dressing, a revamped classic is born!

FOR THE CAESAR DRESSING

- 1 (2-ounce) can anchovies packed in olive oil, drained
- 2 large cloves garlic, peeled and smashed
- 1 tablespoon Worcestershire sauce
- 2 teaspoons lemon juice
- 1 teaspoon Dijon mustard
- ⅛ teaspoon salt
- ⅛ teaspoon ground black pepper
- ⅓ cup olive oil

FOR THE SALAD

- 2 cups romaine lettuce
- 2 cups frisée lettuce
- 2 cups red leaf lettuce
- Whole Grain Rosemary Croutons
- ½ cup grated Parmesan cheese

To make the dressing, in a blender or food processor, pulse the anchovies, garlic, Worcestershire sauce, lemon juice, mustard, and salt and pepper until smooth. Gradually stream in the oil while continuing to pulse until the dressing is completely emulsified. Transfer to a bowl or serving pitcher.

To make the salad, in a large bowl, toss the romaine, frisée, and red leaf lettuces. Add just enough dressing to the greens to lightly coat or serve the dressing on the side. Toss in the croutons (or save to garnish each portion of salad). Divide the salad evenly among 4 serving plates. Top each portion with 2 tablespoons Parmesan and serve.

TIP: Frisée and red leaf lettuce are generally available at most grocery stores, farmers' markets, and farm stands, but if you can't find them, make an all-romaine salad. Just make sure whatever greens you use total 6 cups.

Whole Grain Rosemary Croutons

YIELD: **4 servings**

3 tablespoons olive oil

2 tablespoons minced fresh rosemary leaves

⅛ teaspoon salt

⅛ teaspoon freshly ground black pepper

2½ cups cubed or triangular-sliced whole grain baguette

Preheat the oven to 350°F. Line a baking sheet with aluminum foil.

In a small bowl, combine the oil, rosemary, salt, and pepper. In a large mixing bowl, combine the bread and oil-rosemary mixture and toss to coat completely.

Arrange the bread on the prepared baking sheet in a single, even layer. Toast in the oven for 5 to 6 minutes. Flip the croutons and toast for 5 to 6 minutes more, until golden brown and crispy.

Kewl Chopped Guacamole Salad

YIELD: **6 servings**

A medley of avocado, onion, cilantro, and colorful, flavorful, all-around wonderful red and yellow tomatoes is featured in this deconstructed take on guacamole. As a stand-alone salad or served with chips, this fresh, super-delicious South-of-the-Border-inspired creation couldn't be easier to toss together. Every bite boasts big flavors and some powerful health benefits, too. For instance, avocado is great for your skin, nails, and hair and packs a plentiful punch of vitamins C and K, as well as unsaturated fats, which are the heart-healthy kind.

4 ripe roma tomatoes, cut into ½-inch chunks

1 large yellow tomato, cut into ½-inch chunks

4 ripe avocadoes, cut into ½-inch chunks

1 sweet white onion, cut into ¼-inch chunks

1 bunch fresh cilantro, chopped

Juice of 2 lemons

In a large bowl, gently combine the red and yellow tomatoes, avocadoes, onion, cilantro, and salt and pepper to taste. Add the lemon juice and toss lightly to combine.

Serve for lunch or in a bowl alongside chips for a snack or starter.

Tarragon and Chive Egg Salad

YIELD: **4 servings**

Most egg salads rely on lots of unnecessary mayonnaise, heavy dressings, or excess egg yolks for flavor, but this one features bold chives and tarragon, and crunchy celery instead. I like to serve it piled high onto mini toasts or spooned into tender leaves of Bibb lettuce.

12 large eggs

3 tablespoons low-fat mayonnaise

1 tablespoon Dijon mustard

¼ cup minced fresh chives, plus
    extra for garnish

1½ teaspoons dried tarragon

½ teaspoon sea salt

¼ teaspoon ground black pepper

¾ cup finely diced stalks celery

Place the eggs in a large pot and fill with water to cover. Set over high heat and bring to a boil. Cover and cook for approximately 10 minutes, until hard-boiled. Drain the eggs and transfer to an ice-water bath (a bowl of cold water and ice). Let cool 10 minutes.

Meanwhile, in a small bowl, combine the mayonnaise, mustard, chives, tarragon, salt, and pepper. Mix well to combine. Set aside.

When the eggs are cooled, peel them and discard shells. Dice 6 of the eggs, using both whites and yolks. For the remaining 6 eggs, dice only the whites, discarding the yolks.

In a large mixing bowl, combine the diced eggs and egg whites, celery, and mayonnaise-mustard mixture. Stir until the mixture is smooth and the ingredients uniformly distributed.

Tropical Chicken Salad

YIELD: **6 to 8 servings**

I figured out how to use very little mayonnaise in this chicken salad, instead moistening it with a mix of succulent fruit. And by poaching the chicken breasts in low-sodium chicken broth with celery and carrots, they become super-tender and juicy without any added fat.

2 pounds skinless boneless chicken breasts

32 ounces (4 cups) low-sodium chicken broth

3 stalks celery

2 carrots

1 clove garlic, peeled

¾ cup minced fresh chives, plus extra for garnish

¼ cup low-fat mayonnaise

1 tablespoon freshly squeezed orange juice

¼ teaspoon sea salt

¼ teaspoon ground black pepper

1 cup ¼-inch-cubed fresh pineapple

1 cup ¼-inch-cubed fresh mango

¾ cup almonds, coarsely chopped

Place the chicken breasts in a large pan or Dutch oven. Add the chicken broth, celery, carrots, and garlic. Cover, bring to a boil over high heat, and then immediately reduce to a simmer. Cook 20 minutes, or until the chicken is cooked through and no longer pink. Drain the chicken and set aside to cool. Discard the broth and vegetables.

When the chicken is cool, cut into ½-inch chunks and place in a large bowl.

In a separate bowl, combine the chives, mayonnaise, orange juice, salt, and pepper. Add to the chicken and stir until completely distributed. Stir in the pineapple, mango, and almonds and transfer to serving plates. Garnish with chives and serve.

Tapas-Style Open-Faced Tuna Sandwiches

YIELD: **4 servings**

Straight from the shores of Barcelona, here's my tapas-style take on the popular Catalan combination of tuna and olives. This open-faced sandwich is boldly flavored with fresh dill, chives, and lemon zest. Toast up some whole grain bread, set out a bowl of the lemony tuna salad and the garnishes, and invite friends to make their own!

4 slices 100 percent whole grain sandwich bread, or 1 loaf whole grain crusty bread, sliced

3 (5-ounce) cans white albacore tuna packed in water

3 tablespoons olive oil

¼ teaspoon grated lemon zest

1 tablespoon freshly squeezed lemon juice

2 tablespoons minced fresh chives, plus extra for garnish

2 tablespoons chopped fresh dill, plus extra for garnish

¼ cup pitted olives, thinly sliced into rings, for garnish

Preheat the oven to 350°F. Place the bread on a baking sheet and bake for 5 minutes, until lightly toasted. Set aside.

In a medium bowl, combine the tuna, oil, lemon zest and juice, chives, dill, and salt and pepper to taste. Divide the tuna mixture evenly among the slices of toast. Garnish with extra chives and dill and the sliced olives.

Tapas-Style Open-Faced Salmon Sandwiches with Dill Pesto

YIELD: **4 sandwiches**

Inspired by the time I spent in Spain where smoked salmon is a staple on tapas menus, I've created this single-slice sandwich that makes just as satisfying a lunch as it does supper. Drizzle on the zesty dill "pesto" sauce to add bright flavor.

FOR THE DILL PESTO

- ½ cup packed fresh dill
- 2½ tablespoons Dijon mustard
- ½ teaspoon freshly grated lemon zest
- 2 tablespoons freshly squeezed lemon juice
- 1 tablespoon honey
- ¼ cup olive oil

FOR THE SANDWICHES

- 12 slices smoked salmon
- 4 slices 100 percent whole grain sandwich bread
- 1 English cucumber, sliced into thin rounds
- 4 tablespoons coarsely chopped dill, plus extra for garnish
- 4 tablespoons thinly sliced scallions, both white and green parts, plus extra for garnish

To make the pesto, in a blender or food processor, combine the dill, mustard, lemon zest and juice, and honey and pulse until completely smooth. Gradually add the oil in a stream, while constantly pulsing, until the sauce is thick and completely emulsified.

To assemble the sandwiches, arrange 3 slices of smoked salmon on each slice of bread. Top each with 4 cucumber slices, 1 tablespoon dill, and 1 tablespoon scallions, spreading evenly over the salmon. Drizzle 1 to 2 tablespoons (or to taste) of the dill pesto over each open-faced sandwich. Garnish with extra dill and scallions and serve.

Flatbread Pizza

YIELD: **4 servings**

This delicious pizza conceals a secret flavor weapon: my shallot-garlic-and-oregano-infused olive oil, which I (generously!) brush over the thin dough before baking to give the crispy crust a golden brown hue. If you're in a time crunch, buy premade dough—preferably whole grain—at your local pizza parlor or grocery store. Or, on a leisurely weekend afternoon, turn your kitchen into a pizzeria and whip up your own—midair pizza maestro toss and all!

1 pound whole wheat or multigrain pizza dough, at room temperature

¼ cup olive oil

1 medium shallot, quartered

2 cloves garlic, halved

1 teaspoon dried oregano

1 medium red tomato, sliced into triangular chunks

1 medium yellow tomato, sliced into triangular chunks

8 ounces fresh mozzarella, sliced into large square or triangular chunks

1 cup arugula leaves

¼ cup fresh basil leaves

Preheat the oven to 475°F. Line a large baking sheet with aluminum foil and coat lightly with olive oil.

Lightly dust a rolling pin and cutting board with flour. Roll the dough out to an even, flat rectangle approximately 14 by 9 inches. Ensure that there are no holes.

In a food processor, combine the oil, shallot, garlic, and oregano and pulse until smooth. Brush the paste liberally over the dough, reserving some for the toppings. Carefully transfer the dough to the baking sheet. Top evenly with the tomatoes and cheese and brush lightly with the remaining paste.

Bake the pizza for 14 minutes, until the dough is puffed and golden and the cheese begins to bubble. Top evenly with the arugula and basil and bake 3 minutes more, until the arugula is wilted and the dough is crispy.

Cut into 10 slices and serve.

Chapter 3
Mains

WHAT'S FOR DINNER? Most days, before I've even had my first bite of breakfast, I'm already thinking about what I want for dinner. For some reason, deciding what to make for dinner always seems to be a little more challenging than any other meal. Maybe it's because it requires a little extra planning, or possibly because it may be difficult to please everyone in the family.

With even the best intentions, gathering around the dinner table seems to be just out of reach for so many, and usually for understandable reasons. We're so busy juggling school, work commitments, hours of homework, and after-school activities that there's little room or time in the day to make plans for what always seems like the **biggest meal of the day.** But just as breakfast is essential to fueling you in the morning, and lunch is a must for sustaining you through the day, dinner is not only an ideal time to refuel, but also the time to wind down with family or friends. There's no better time to engage, connect, or *reconnect.* So, in order to make it happen in my house, I've developed a few guidelines for myself—and you—that can help get a nutritious meal on the table every night.

PLAN AHEAD. To eliminate the daily planning dilemma, schedule a week's worth of meals in one sitting. And don't do it alone. Enlist your family members to help you plan six or seven dinner menus; that way, everyone can contribute his or her **favorite dishes** (Rule: They've got to be good for you!), and you can draw up a shopping list to ensure you have everything on hand for the next 7 days.

STOCK YOUR PANTRY, FREEZER, AND FRIDGE. Half of the battle when it comes to cooking healthfully is having the ingredients you need on hand. Luckily, it's easy to be successful on that front. I know that when a midweek trip to the grocery store is required in order to get dinner on the table, it is unlikely that it will actually happen. In the past, with both of my parents at the office, it was pretty common to find our fridge and freezer understocked (if not well on the road to empty!). Nowadays, our freezer is filled with frozen fruits, vegetables, chicken, lean turkey, and salmon fillets. The pantry is home to staples like whole grain pasta; canned tomatoes and beans; boxed chicken and vegetable broths (all low-sodium, of course); and tons of exotic, flavorful spices, dried herbs, seasonings, and condiments. For a rundown of pantry essentials to keep on hand, check out my list on page 202. Putting together a meal is stress-free when every single ingredient you need is already at your fingertips.

DOUBLE-BATCH YOUR DINNERS. One for now and one for later! No downsides here. For instance, check out my easy yet super-flavorful and moist Turkey Meatballs (page 89) paired with hearty Italian Marinara Sauce (page 90). Make a double batch of the meatballs and some extra sauce (who doesn't love that?), and freeze them for later. Then, farther down the line (maybe tomorrow, this weekend, or later in the month), thaw, pour into a pan, and you've got a delicious dinner in a flash!

CREATE A WEEKLY THEME NIGHT. Some of the best dinners our family shares are themed around a particular food or cuisine. Friday nights have officially been declared pizza night, and we love to customize our own array of essential, can't-live-(or eat pizza)-without-'em toppings. Taco night is another favorite (*ique divertido!*), so I've tailored the typical taco to include turkey layered with seasoned beans rather than the refried version, all wrapped in a whole wheat tortilla (See my Turkey Tacos recipe on page 94). It's proof that there's always a successful solution to enjoy the dishes we love the most, and to pull it off both healthfully—and kewly.

Crab Cakes

YIELD: **4 crab cakes**

Transport the flavors of the New England coast to your kitchen with these perfect crab cakes. Lemon, parsley, and tarragon give these crispy-on-the-outside, succulent-on-the-inside cakes bright, vivid flavors. Instead of using just mayonnaise to bind the lump crabmeat with the other ingredients, I've lightened up the mix with egg whites and a little Dijon mustard.

2 teaspoons plus 1 tablespoon olive oil, divided

1 medium shallot, minced

1 scallion, white and green parts, thinly sliced

2 medium cloves garlic, minced

1 cup coarse fresh whole wheat bread crumbs, divided*

½ pound fresh crab claw meat

½ pound fresh jumbo lump crabmeat

¼ cup minced red bell pepper

¼ cup minced yellow bell pepper

¼ cup minced celery

¼ cup minced fresh flat-leaf parsley

2 tablespoons minced fresh tarragon

¼ cup low-fat mayonnaise

1½ teaspoons grated lemon zest, divided

2 tablespoons freshly squeezed lemon juice

2 large egg whites

1 tablespoon Dijon mustard

¾ teaspoon sea salt, divided

⅛ teaspoon ground red pepper

1 teaspoon garlic powder

Preheat the oven to 375°F. Line a baking sheet with aluminum foil and lightly coat the foil with oil.

Heat 2 teaspoons of the oil in a sauté pan over medium heat. Add the shallot and scallion and sauté 2 to 3 minutes, until softened. Add the garlic and cook 1 minute, stirring often.

Transfer to a large mixing bowl and add ¾ cup of the bread crumbs, both types of crabmeat, the peppers, celery, parsley, and tarragon. Stir to combine, being careful to avoid breaking up the crabmeat as much as possible.

(continued)

*TIP: Homemade bread crumbs are key here—and they're so simple to make. Put a few slices of whole wheat bread in a food processor or blender and pulse until the texture resembles coarse crumbs.

In a separate bowl, combine the mayonnaise, 1 teaspoon of the lemon zest and juice, egg whites, mustard, $\frac{1}{2}$ teaspoon salt, and the red pepper. Mix thoroughly.

Add the wet ingredients to the dry and mix until completely combined and the bread crumbs are moistened, taking care not to break up the crab. Using your hands, shape the mixture into four 1-inch-thick patties.

Heat the remaining 1 tablespoon oil in a sauté pan over medium heat. Add 2 of the crab-cakes and sear 2 minutes, until golden brown. Gently flip the cakes and cook until browned on the other side, 2 minutes, taking care not to break them apart. Transfer to the baking sheet. Repeat with the 2 remaining cakes.

In a small bowl, combine the remaining $\frac{1}{4}$ cup bread crumbs, $\frac{1}{4}$ teaspoon salt, $\frac{1}{2}$ teaspoon lemon zest, and the garlic powder. Sprinkle over the crab cakes, gently compacting them. Bake for 6 to 8 minutes, or until cooked through completely.

Grilled Swordfish Steaks with Sautéed Mustard Greens

YIELD: **4 servings**

Juicy medallions of swordfish on a bed of pungent mustard greens make for a perfectly balanced combination of flavors. Mustard greens, a relative of kale and collard greens, lend a peppery note that echoes the pungent flavors of the familiar condiment that shares their namesake.

4 swordfish steaks, about 5 ounces each

3 tablespoons olive oil, divided

1 tablespoon balsamic vinegar

2 shallots, peeled and quartered

2 cloves garlic, coarsely chopped

1½ tablespoons chopped fresh flat-leaf parsley

¼ teaspoon sea salt, plus extra to taste

¼ teaspoon ground black pepper, plus extra to taste

2 bunches mustard greens,* stems removed and coarsely chopped

Place the swordfish steaks in a wide, flat baking dish. Lightly pierce all over on both sides with a fork.

In a blender or food processor, pulse 2 tablespoons of the oil with the vinegar, shallots, garlic, parsley, ¼ teaspoon salt, and ¼ teaspoon pepper until completely smooth. Pour evenly over the swordfish, cover, and marinate approximately 3 hours in the refrigerator.

Preheat the grill to medium or heat a grill pan over medium heat on the stovetop. Place the swordfish on the grill and cook 2 minutes. Rotate each steak 90 degrees (a quarter turn) and cook 2 to 3 minutes more. Flip the steaks and cook until firm and cooked through, 5 minutes more. Keep warm.

Heat the remaining 1 tablespoon oil in a large skillet over medium-high heat. Add the greens and season with salt and pepper to taste. Sauté until tender and wilted, about 5 minutes.

Divide the greens evenly among 4 serving plates and top each with a swordfish steak.

*TIP: If you can't find mustard greens, feel free to substitute kale or collard greens.

Vietnamese Summer Rolls with Pan-Asian Dipping Sauce

YIELD: **8 spring rolls, serving 4**

Summer rolls, a Vietnamese classic, are so much fun and really easy to make. Plus, they score points visually, with the translucent rice paper wrappers showing off the vivid, fresh fillings within. You'll love arranging all of the ingredients assembly line–style, and then letting friends and family fill their own rolls aa they wish.

8 individual rice paper wrappers

3 carrots, peeled and cut into matchsticks

1 avocado, thinly sliced

1 English cucumber, peeled and cut into matchsticks

24 medium shrimp, shelled, deveined, cooked,* and halved lengthwise

½ cup cilantro leaves

2 teaspoons sesame seeds

FOR THE DIPPING SAUCE

3 tablespoons rice vinegar

2 tablespoons reduced-sodium soy sauce

1½ tablespoons coarsely chopped fresh lemongrass

1 tablespoon coarsely chopped peeled fresh ginger

1 teaspoon coarsely chopped garlic

1 teaspoon canola oil

Soak the wrappers in a bowl of warm water for 5 seconds (or according to package instructions) to rehydrate. Follow the steps (opposite) to make the rolls.

To prepare the dipping sauce, combine the vinegar, soy sauce, lemongrass, ginger, garlic, and oil in the bowl of a food processor. Pulse until combined and completely smooth, 1 to 2 minutes. Season to taste with salt.

Serve the spring rolls with dipping sauce on the side.

*TIP: Use precooked shrimp or cook your own by poaching fresh shrimp in boiling water for about 5 minutes, until firm and pink—but not overdone! Remember, shrimp cook super-fast, so keep an eye on them. If using frozen, be sure to allow for thawing time.

1 Working on one roll at a time, set a wrapper on a cutting board or flat dish. In the center, arrange the carrot, avocado, and cucumber. Top with 6 shrimp halves, 1 tablespoon cilantro, and ¼ teaspoon sesame seeds.

2 Begin rolling the wrapper around the filling.

3 Fold the right and left edges in to seal the ends.

4 Continue rolling the wrapper into a cylindrical shape, then lightly moisten the edge to seal it. Be careful not to break the wrapper or leave any interior ingredients exposed.

Shrimp Stir-Fry with Kewl Ginger-Lemongrass "Special Sauce"

YIELD: **4 servings**

My kewl twist on a typical stir-fry cuts down on the excessive oil and salt that you might encounter by ordering off the delivery menu. Enhanced by my "special sauce," this dish is bursting with citrusy notes of lemongrass and spicy undertones of ginger.

FOR THE SPECIAL SAUCE AND SHRIMP

¾ cup rice vinegar

½ cup reduced-sodium soy sauce

1 tablespoon plus 1 teaspoon canola oil

¼ cup plus 2 tablespoons coarsely chopped fresh stalk lemongrass

¼ cup coarsely chopped peeled fresh ginger

1 tablespoon plus 1 teaspoon coarsely chopped garlic

¼ teaspoon sea salt

1 pound medium shrimp, peeled and deveined

FOR THE STIR-FRY

1 (8-ounce) package 100 percent whole wheat udon noodles

2 tablespoons canola oil, divided

1 cup shiitake mushrooms, stems removed and caps sliced into strips

½ cup sliced bok choy

½ cup julienned yellow bell pepper

½ cup julienned red bell pepper

½ cup shredded carrots

½ cup water chestnuts, sliced

½ cup canned baby corn, drained

½ cup snow peas

½ cup coarsely chopped cilantro, plus extra for garnish

¼ cup cashews, toasted (see page 37) and coarsely chopped, for garnish (optional)

To make the sauce, combine the vinegar, soy sauce, oil, lemongrass, ginger, garlic, and salt in a blender or food processor and pulse until completely smooth, 1 to 2 minutes. Transfer to a plastic zip-top bag set in a glass bowl or baking dish. Add the shrimp, seal the bag, and marinate in the refrigerator for 20 minutes.

(continued)

Cook the noodles in a large pot of boiling water until al dente, 10 to 12 minutes (or according to package directions).

While the noodles are cooking, heat a large stovetop or electric wok to medium high. Once hot, add 1 tablespoon of the oil, followed by the marinated shrimp and approximately half of the sauce (1 cup) from the plastic bag. Cook, stirring often, until the shrimp is just cooked through and slightly pink, 3 to 5 minutes. Remove to a dish and keep warm.

Add the remaining 1 tablespoon oil to the wok. Add the mushrooms, bok choy, peppers, carrots, water chestnuts, baby corn, snow peas, and remaining 1 cup sauce, and stir-fry until the vegetables are crisp-tender and the sauce has thickened slightly, 3 to 4 minutes. Stir in the cilantro.

Divide the noodles among 4 plates. Top with the stir-fried vegetables and the shrimp. Garnish with cilantro and toasted cashews, if desired.

Seafood-Stuffed Shells

YIELD: **4 to 5 servings**

Whenever I make this, I'm reminded of my trips to Italy—Venice and Rome in particular. Jumbo pasta shells are stuffed with a mouthwatering mixture of shrimp and scallops simmered in a quick tomato sauce seasoned with garlic, oregano, and basil. It's a healthier version of the traditional pasta dish in which the fish are usually swimming in boatloads of butter with bread crumbs and heavy cream. Parmesan packs a lot of flavor in just tiny amounts, making it a delicious garnish for almost any pasta dish.

16 to 20 uncooked jumbo pasta shells

1 tablespoon olive oil

3 medium shallots, diced

2 cloves garlic, minced

1 (28-ounce) can crushed tomatoes

2 tablespoons coarsely chopped fresh oregano

1 tablespoon coarsely chopped fresh basil

1 teaspoon salt

½ teaspoon freshly ground black pepper

6 ounces cooked bay scallops*

6 ounces cooked small shrimp*

¼ cup plus 2 tablespoons freshly grated Parmesan cheese

Cook the pasta shells according to the package instructions. Drain and set aside.

Heat the oil in a large saucepan over medium heat. Add the shallots and sauté until softened, 3 to 4 minutes. Add the garlic and cook 1 minute. Add the tomatoes, oregano, basil, salt, and pepper and simmer, stirring occasionally, until slightly reduced and thickened, 15 to 20 minutes.

Preheat the oven to 350°F. Lightly coat a large baking dish with olive oil.

In a medium bowl, mix the scallops and shrimp with approximately half of the tomato sauce. Stuff each pasta shell with the seafood mixture until full. Arrange the shells in a single, tight layer in the prepared baking dish, allowing the shells to touch and using 2 dishes if necessary. Pour the remaining tomato sauce over the shells and spread to cover evenly.

Bake the shells, uncovered, for 30 minutes, until heated through and slightly crispy. Sprinkle with the Parmesan and bake 5 minutes, until the cheese is browned.

*TIP: If you purchase your scallops or shrimp uncooked, bring a pot of water to a boil, add the seafood, and cook for 5 minutes. Drain well.

Mussels Marinara

YIELD: **2 main dish servings or 4 appetizer servings**

A classic that's delicious and fun to eat, this shellfish dish features a spectacular, crimson marinara seasoned with fragrant parsley, basil, and oregano—ideal for sopping up with a fresh slice of crusty Italian bread.

2 tablespoons olive oil

1 medium sweet onion, diced

2 cloves garlic, minced

1 (14.5-ounce) can crushed tomatoes

2 tablespoons minced fresh flat-leaf parsley, plus extra for garnish

1 tablespoon minced fresh basil

1 tablespoon minced fresh oregano

1 pinch crushed red-pepper flakes

¼ teaspoon salt

1 pound mussels,* rinsed and debearded

⅓ cup water

Heat the oil in a large sauté pan with high sides over medium-high heat. Add the onion and sauté until translucent, 6 to 8 minutes. Add the garlic and sauté 1 to 2 minutes. Add the tomatoes, parsley, basil, oregano, red-pepper flakes, salt, and pepper to taste. Simmer, stirring occasionally, until thickened and aromatic, about 5 minutes.

Add the mussels and water. Cover and cook until the shells open, about 5 minutes.

For an appetizer or shared main course, transfer the mussels to a serving bowl along with a few spoonfuls of the marinara sauce and garnish with parsley. Alternatively, serve the mussels over 2 individual servings of hot pasta along with several spoonfuls of the marinara sauce and garnish.

*TIP: Before cooking, discard any mussels with open or cracked shells; only use those that are tightly sealed. After cooking, discard any mussels that remain closed.

Seared Sesame Tuna with Sautéed Snow Peas and Mushrooms

YIELD: **4 servings**

This sushi bar staple is super-easy to make at home. Lemongrass and fresh ginger infuse the fragrant marinade, and a coating of black and white sesame seeds gives every bite a distinctive crunch.

FOR THE MARINADE

- ¼ cup coarsely chopped peeled fresh ginger
- ¼ cup plus 2 tablespoons rice vinegar
- ¼ cup reduced-sodium soy sauce
- 3 tablespoons coarsely chopped lemongrass
- 2 teaspoons canola oil
- 2 teaspoons coarsely chopped garlic
- ¼ teaspoon sea salt

FOR THE TUNA STEAKS

- 4 ahi tuna steaks, about 5 ounces each
- ¼ cup plus 2 tablespoons black sesame seeds
- ¼ cup plus 2 tablespoons white sesame seeds
- 2 tablespoons canola oil, divided, plus extra if needed
- 2 cups chopped mushrooms*
- 2 cups snow peas

Combine the marinade ingredients in a blender or food processor and pulse until smooth. Place the steaks in a wide baking dish and pierce all over on both sides with a fork. Pour in half of the marinade, cover, and refrigerate at least 1 hour. Reserve the remaining marinade.

Combine the black and white sesame seeds on a shallow platter. In a large sauté pan, heat 1 tablespoon of the oil over medium-high heat. Using tongs, dip 2 steaks into the sesame seeds to cover both sides. Sear until white around the edges and rare in the middle, 2 to 3 minutes per side. Remove to a dish. Repeat with the remaining oil and steaks.

If necessary, lightly coat the same pan with oil. Add the mushrooms, snow peas, and the reserved marinade and cook until crisp-tender, 5 to 8 minutes. Season with salt and pepper and serve with the tuna steaks.

*TIP: What kind of mushrooms? You pick! For this recipe, the basic button mushroom is the most accessible, but feel free to experiment with more exotic varieties such as oyster or king trumpet.

Baked Fish Sticks with Tartar Sauce

YIELD: **4 to 6 servings**

Pick up one of these crisp-tender sticks of flaky, baked—not fried—fish, dip it into the *herbal*icious tartar sauce, and fulfill your craving for crunch!

3 large egg whites

1 cup panko bread crumbs

1 cup crushed unsweetened cornflakes cereal

¼ cup minced fresh flat-leaf parsley

2 teaspoons dried dill weed

1 tablespoon onion powder

2 teaspoons garlic powder

1 teaspoon mustard powder

½ teaspoon sea salt

½ teaspoon ground black pepper

1½ pounds tilapia fillets, cut into 1- by 4-inch strips

FOR THE TARTAR SAUCE

¾ cup low-fat mayonnaise

3 tablespoons light sour cream

2 tablespoons minced sweet onion

1 tablespoon minced dill pickles

1 teaspoon minced fresh flat-leaf parsley

1 teaspoon dried dill weed (or 1 tablespoon minced fresh)

1 teaspoon dried tarragon (or ¾ teaspoon minced fresh)

1 teaspoon Dijon mustard

½ teaspoon Worcestershire sauce

¼ teaspoon sea salt

Preheat the oven to 450°F. Line a baking sheet with aluminum foil and lightly coat with oil.

Lightly beat the egg whites in a medium bowl. In a wide baking dish, combine the bread crumbs, cereal, parsley, dill weed, onion powder, garlic powder, mustard powder, salt, and pepper. Using tongs, thoroughly coat the tilapia strips first with the egg whites, followed by the bread crumbs.* Place on the baking sheet and bake until golden brown and crispy and the fish is cooked through, 20 to 25 minutes.

Meanwhile, combine the tartar sauce ingredients in a medium serving bowl and mix well until evenly distributed. Serve beside the warm fish sticks.

*TIP: When using the tongs, be sure to intermittently wash and dry them to prevent a buildup of crumbs.

Fish Tacos with Mango Salsa

YIELD: **6 tacos**

Fresh flavors and a bright, colorful filling make these tacos the perfect feast for a family get-together! To boost fiber, say adios to deep-fried taco shells and use soft whole wheat tortillas instead.

FOR THE FISH AND MARINADE

- 4 skin-on red snapper fillets,* about 6 ounces each
- 3 tablespoons minced cilantro
- 1 scallion, white and green parts, minced
- 2 cloves garlic, minced
- ¼ cup orange juice
- 2 tablespoons lime juice
- 2 tablespoons olive oil
- ¼ teaspoon sea salt
- ⅛ teaspoon ground black pepper

FOR THE SALSA

- 2 roma tomatoes, seeded and chopped
- 2 mangoes, peeled, pitted, and diced
- 1 English cucumber, peeled and diced
- 1 tablespoon plus 1 teaspoon coarsely chopped cilantro, plus extra for garnish
- 2 tablespoons lime juice
- ⅛ teaspoon sea salt
- 2 avocadoes, diced
- 6 (6-inch) tortillas (100 percent whole wheat)

To marinate the fish, place the fillets in a baking dish and pierce with a fork all over on both sides. Combine the marinade ingredients in a medium bowl, pour over the fish, cover with plastic wrap, and refrigerate 1 hour.

Preheat the grill to medium high or heat a grill pan over medium-high heat on the stovetop. Grill the fish, flesh side down, about 5 minutes. Using tongs, flip the fillets over and cook until opaque and cooked through, 2 to 3 minutes. Transfer to a platter, remove the skin, and flake the fish with a fork.

Combine the tomatoes, mangoes, cucumber, 1 tablespoon plus 1 teaspoon cilantro, lime juice, and salt in a medium bowl and mix. Add the avocado and gently toss. Divide the fish evenly among the 6 tortillas. Spoon the salsa over each and garnish with cilantro.

*TIP: Other fish taco–friendly options include mahi mahi and tilapia. The result will be light, flaky, fresh, and delicious!

Chicken Pad Thai

YIELD: **4 servings**

Most restaurant versions of this Thai classic are loaded with excess oil and sodium, but my take relies on a combination of fresh garlic, ginger, and cilantro to amp up the flavor. This is one of those straightforward dishes that you will commit to memory after you've made it a few times. Chances are you will, because it's among the most satisfying one-bowl meals around.

8 ounces dried rice noodles

1 pound chicken breasts, cut into ¼ inch cubes

¼ cup plus 1 tablespoon lime juice, divided

3 tablespoons creamy peanut butter

2 tablespoons reduced-sodium soy sauce

2 tablespoons honey

1 tablespoon chili sauce

1 tablespoon water

2 tablespoons canola oil, divided

1 large egg

2 large egg whites

1 tablespoon minced fresh ginger

2 cloves garlic, minced

¼ teaspoon sea salt

¼ teaspoon ground black pepper

1½ cups bean sprouts

½ cup thinly sliced scallions, plus extra for garnish

½ cup coarsely chopped cilantro, plus extra for garnish

4 tablespoons toasted unsalted peanuts

Soak the noodles in hot water until al dente. Drain and set aside.

In a medium bowl, toss the chicken with ¼ cup of the lime juice. Cover with plastic wrap or aluminum foil and marinate 1 hour in the refrigerator.

In a small bowl, combine the remaining 1 tablespoon lime juice, the peanut butter, soy sauce, honey, chili sauce, and water. Set aside.

In a large sauté pan, heat 2 teaspoons of the oil over medium-high heat. Lightly beat together the egg and egg whites, then add to the pan. Cook, scrambling quickly with a spatula, about 1 minute. Remove to a plate and set aside.

(continued)

Add 1 tablespoon of the oil to the pan. Drain the chicken of excess lime juice and sauté in the pan until cooked through, 5 minutes. Remove to a plate.

Add the remaining 1 teaspoon oil to the pan. Add the ginger and cook 1 minute, stirring often. Add the garlic, salt, and pepper and cook 1 minute, continuing to stir. Add the bean sprouts and cook until slightly wilted, 3 to 4 minutes. Add the chili-peanut sauce and simmer about 1 minute. Add the noodles and cook 1 to 2 minutes, stirring often.

Fold the scrambled eggs and chicken back into the pan, along with the scallions and cilantro. Cook 1 minute. Divide the mixture evenly among 4 plates or bowls. Garnish each with 1 tablespoon peanuts, scallions, and cilantro.

Moo Shoo Chicken Wraps

YIELD: **8 wraps**

Sunday night means Chinese food in our house! Rather than ordering in, we whip up this quintessential take-out staple, but without all of the fat and sodium that hide in the version you get from the Chinese restaurant.

1 pound skinless boneless chicken breasts, sliced into thin strips

¼ teaspoon garlic powder

½ cup low-sodium chicken broth, divided

1½ tablespoons canola oil, divided

1 tablespoon minced fresh ginger

2 cloves garlic, minced

¼ cup reduced-sodium soy sauce

1 cup sliced button mushrooms

1 cup bamboo shoots

1 cup shredded carrots

1 cup bite-sized broccoli florets

¼ cup thinly sliced scallions, white and green parts, plus extra for garnish

2 tablespoons hoisin sauce

8 (6-inch) tortillas (100 percent whole wheat), warmed/toasted lightly if desired

Heat a large sauté pan or wok over medium heat. Season the chicken with salt and pepper, and the garlic powder. Add ¼ cup of the broth plus 1 tablespoon of the oil to the pan. Add the chicken and cook, stirring occasionally, until cooked through, 8 to 10 minutes. Remove the chicken from the pan and set aside.

Add the remaining ½ tablespoon oil to the pan. Add the ginger and garlic and sauté about 1 minute, until lightly browned. Add the soy sauce and remaining ¼ cup broth. Add the mushrooms, bamboo shoots, carrots, and broccoli. Cook, stirring often, until softened, 7 to 8 minutes.

Return the chicken to the pan along with the scallions and hoisin sauce. Cook, stirring, until heated through, 2 to 3 minutes more. Divide evenly among the tortillas and roll each tightly into a cylindrical shape. Garnish with sliced scallions and serve.

Rustic Roasted Chicken

YIELD: **4 to 6 servings**

This ultimate comfort food is a weeknight staple in my house; it couldn't be easier to pull together. Juicy lemons, herbs like thyme and parsley, and fresh garlic not only fill the cavity of the chicken, but their aromas will permeate the entire kitchen, too. Brush on the tangy mustard rub, set your timer, and let your oven do the rest. Serve it with my Roasted Fingerling Potatoes (page 134), Apple-Pear Compote with Vanilla Bean (page 142), and a light green salad alongside, and dinner is a go!

FOR THE WET RUB

¼ cup olive oil

2 tablespoons Dijon mustard

2 tablespoons minced fresh thyme

2 tablespoons minced fresh flat-leaf parsley

2 cloves garlic, minced

½ teaspoon sea salt

¼ teaspoon ground black pepper

FOR THE CHICKEN

1 fresh organic whole chicken, about 4 pounds

1 lemon, halved

3 cloves garlic, peeled and halved

15 sprigs fresh flat-leaf parsley

15 sprigs fresh thyme

1 cup low-sodium chicken broth

To make the rub, combine all the ingredients in a bowl and mix well.

Preheat the oven to 350°F. Rinse the chicken inside and out and pat dry. Season inside the body cavity with salt and pepper. Place the lemon halves, garlic cloves, and parsley and thyme sprigs in the cavity. Place the chicken in a roasting pan or baking dish. Spread the rub evenly over the chicken, covering all exposed skin and meat.

Pour the broth around the chicken in the pan. Roast for 80 minutes, or until the internal temperature of the chicken, where legs meet breasts, is 165°F and the chicken juices run clear when the meat is pierced by a fork. Let rest 5 minutes before carving.

Grilled Garlic and Herb Chicken

YIELD: **6 servings**

Whether you're planning your next tailgate or gathering friends and family around the TV, these savory wings and legs are just the ticket. My prepared marinade is so much better for you than jarred BBQ sauce; it's lower in sodium and contains no sugar, preservatives, or additives. Instead, you'll find the robust flavors of garlic, basil, and oregano. Serve these smoky grilled wings and legs with my Butternut Squash Fries (page 131).

½ cup low-sodium chicken broth

3 tablespoons olive oil

1 tablespoon lemon juice

3 tablespoons minced garlic

2 tablespoons minced fresh basil

2 tablespoons minced fresh oregano

¼ teaspoon sea salt

¼ teaspoon ground black pepper

4 pounds chicken wings and legs

In a bowl, combine the chicken broth, olive oil, lemon juice, garlic, basil, oregano, salt, and pepper to make the marinade.

Place the chicken wings and legs in a large baking dish. Pour the marinade over the chicken, cover with plastic wrap or aluminum foil, and marinate in the refrigerator for 1 hour.

Preheat the grill to medium or heat a grill pan over medium heat on the stovetop. Coat the grates lightly with olive oil. Working in batches (if necessary), grill the chicken, turning every 4 to 5 minutes with tongs, until cooked through completely (the thickest parts register 165°F on a meat thermometer), 20 to 25 minutes.

Crispy Chicken Wings and Legs

YIELD: **4 servings**

This classic comfort food is hard to take comfort in when you're trying to eat healthfully, I know. So I took it out of the deep fryer altogether and put it on a baking sheet, after coating the wings and legs with a delicious mixture of panko bread crumbs, herbs, and spices.

4 egg whites

3 cups panko bread crumbs

2 tablespoons minced fresh rosemary

2 teaspoons garlic powder

1½ teaspoons red-pepper flakes

1 teaspoon onion powder

1 teaspoon mustard powder

½ teaspoon sea salt

½ teaspoon ground black pepper

3 pounds assorted chicken wings and legs

Preheat the oven to 475°F. Line 2 large baking sheets with aluminum foil and coat lightly with olive oil cooking spray.

Place the egg whites in a bowl. Set aside. In a wide baking dish, combine the bread crumbs, rosemary, garlic powder, red-pepper flakes, onion powder, mustard powder, salt, and pepper. Using tongs, dip each chicken leg/wing into the egg whites and thoroughly coat. Dip next into the bread crumb mixture and cover completely. Transfer to the baking sheets.

Bake 30 to 35 minutes, until the chicken is browned well. Reduce the oven temperature to 375°F and bake 10 minutes more, until the chicken is cooked through.

Serve with Ranch Dip (page 168).

Chicken Fajitas

YIELD: **6 fajitas**

I love to cook with spice and herb mixtures because nothing transforms a dish quite so easily as they do. Here, chili powder, cumin seeds, and paprika season a mix of multicolored bell peppers, caramelized onions, and moist, tender chicken in sizzling fajitas. Assemble the basic fajitas, then set up a toppings bar with salsa, guacamole, and shredded cheese so guests can create their own.

3 cloves garlic, minced

1½ teaspoons whole cumin seeds

¾ teaspoon chili powder

¾ teaspoon ground paprika

½ teaspoon sea salt

½ teaspoon ground black pepper

1 pound skinless boneless chicken breasts, sliced into thin strips

Olive oil, for the pan

½ medium sweet white onion, sliced into thin strips

2 medium bell peppers (red, yellow, and/or green), sliced into thin strips

Garlic powder

6 (8-inch) tortillas (100 percent whole grain)

Toppings of choice, such as shredded lettuce, shredded reduced-fat Cheddar cheese, reduced-fat sour cream, reduced-fat guacamole, salsa, and diced tomato

In a small bowl, combine the garlic, cumin, chili powder, ground paprika, salt, and black pepper. Put in a large resealable plastic bag. Add the chicken strips, seal, and shake the bag until the chicken is uniformly coated.

Lightly coat a large sauté pan with olive oil and set over medium-high heat. When the oil begins to shimmer, add the onion and peppers and season with garlic powder to taste. Sauté until the vegetables have softened slightly, 5 to 7 minutes.

(continued)

Push the vegetables to one side of the pan with a spoon or spatula. Lightly coat the exposed area of the pan with additional olive oil and add the seasoned chicken strips. Cook, turning the strips once, until browned and completely cooked through, 3 to 4 minutes per side.

While the chicken is cooking, arrange the tortillas on a large work surface, such as a cutting board. Place your toppings in small bowls.

To construct an individual fajita, place desired toppings in the center of a tortilla. Next, add a layer of the sautéed onions and peppers, followed by approximately 8 strips of chicken. Carefully roll the wrap into a cylinder, place seam-side down, and slice in half. Repeat to make 6 wraps. Serve with the additional toppings.

TIP: My grandparents gave me a spice rack a few years ago—the first kitchen gift I'd ever received. It's one of those great racks with a series of glass "test tubes," each one holding a different spice. Many of my recipes were inspired by my obsession with these herbs and spices—I love sniffing, sampling, and combining them to create new flavors. Putting herbs and spices in clearly marked containers is a good idea if you want to be efficient—and inspired—in the kitchen (no searching in the pantry for that elusive jar!).

Turkey Chili

YIELD: **6 servings**

If you're coming in from the cold, there's nothing more comforting (or more effective at thawing you out) than a simmering pot of hearty, homemade chili on the stove. Filled with tons of good-for-you ingredients like satisfying beans and nutrient-rich tomatoes, this turkey chili could not be healthier. I love to top it off with crushed tortilla chips for a bit of crunch.

2 tablespoons olive oil

1 sweet onion, diced

½ cup diced red bell pepper

⅓ cup diced, seeded poblano chile pepper

1 serrano chile pepper, seeded and diced

2 tablespoons tomato paste

2 tablespoons minced fresh oregano

1 tablespoon chili powder

1 teaspoon minced garlic

1 teaspoon whole cumin seeds

½ teaspoon paprika

¾ teaspoon sea salt

¼ teaspoon ground black pepper

1¼ pounds lean ground turkey meat

1 (14-ounce) can red kidney beans, drained and rinsed

1 (28-ounce) can diced or crushed tomatoes

½ cup thinly sliced scallions, plus extra for garnish

¾ cup grated reduced-fat Cheddar cheese

Crushed toasted whole grain tortilla chips, for garnish (optional)

Heat the oil in a large pot or Dutch oven over medium heat. Add the onion, red bell pepper, poblano pepper, and serrano pepper and sauté until lightly browned, 10 to 15 minutes.

Stir in the tomato paste, oregano, chili powder, garlic, cumin seeds, paprika, salt, and pepper. Add the ground turkey and cook, stirring and breaking up the meat with a spatula to crumble, until the turkey is browned and completely cooked through, 6 to 8 minutes.

Stir in the kidney beans and tomatoes and simmer 10 minutes. Add the scallions and cook, stirring occasionally, until the scallions are tender, 3 to 4 minutes.

Divide the chili evenly among 6 bowls. Garnish each serving with sliced scallions, 2 tablespoons Cheddar cheese, and crushed tortilla chips, if desired.

Mini Chicken Parm Meatballs

YIELD: **4 main dish servings or approximately 6 appetizer servings**

Ground chicken flavored with carrots, onions, and mushrooms comprises the meatballs in these super-satisfying skewers. They can be served atop a tangle of whole wheat spaghetti in marinara sauce for a main course, or as hors d'oeuvres on bamboo skewers.

¾ cup plus 2 tablespoons whole wheat panko bread crumbs, divided

½ cup plus 2 tablespoons grated Parmesan cheese, divided

½ cup finely grated carrots

½ cup diced sweet onion

½ cup minced white button mushrooms

1 clove garlic, minced

2 tablespoons chopped fresh thyme

2 tablespoons chopped fresh flat-leaf parsley

¾ teaspoon sea salt

½ teaspoon ground black pepper

1 pound lean ground chicken

Marinara Sauce (page 90), for serving and dipping

13 bamboo skewers

Preheat the oven to 400°F. Line a baking sheet with foil and lightly coat the foil with olive oil.

In a large mixing bowl, combine ½ cup of the bread crumbs, ¼ cup of the cheese, the carrots, onion, mushrooms, garlic, thyme, parsley, salt, and pepper. Stir until completely combined. Add the ground chicken and mix with your hands until all ingredients are evenly distributed but not overworked; the resulting mixture should be supple. (Overmixing can cause the meat to break down, making it less conducive to forming meatballs.)

Divide the meat mixture in half. Divide each half in half. Repeat once more, creating a total of 8 portions. Working from 1 portion, remove about one-fifth of the mixture and roll it into a 1-inch sphere in the palms of your clean hands. Place on the prepared baking sheet. Repeat to make 5 miniature meatballs from each portion, for approximately 40 meatballs total. Bake the meatballs for 12 minutes, or until the tops are golden brown and the chicken is cooked through, or very nearly so.

While the meatballs are baking, combine the remaining bread crumbs and cheese in a bowl. Remove the pan from the oven and preheat the broiler. Sprinkle the tops of the meatballs with the bread crumb/cheese mixture, evenly distributing the topping over all meatballs. Place the baking sheet on the center rack in the oven and broil the meatballs 2 to 3 minutes, until the topping has browned and the cheese has melted. Let cool slightly, about 5 minutes.

To serve, thread 3 meatballs on each skewer. Serve with Marinara Sauce on the side for dipping. Alternatively, toss the marinara with cooked whole wheat spaghetti and top with 3 meatball skewers.

Turkey Meatballs
with Marinara Sauce

YIELD: **3 to 4 servings (3 to 4 meatballs per serving)**

Lean ground turkey makes fantastic meatballs when combined with grated zucchini—the secret to imparting just the right amount of moisture.

1 pound spaghetti

1 pound lean ground turkey

2 large egg whites, lightly beaten

⅓ cup whole wheat panko bread crumbs

½ cup diced sweet onion

½ cup finely grated zucchini

¼ cup grated Parmesan cheese

2 tablespoons chopped fresh thyme

2 tablespoons chopped fresh flat-leaf parsley

1 clove garlic, minced

¾ teaspoon sea salt

½ teaspoon ground black pepper

Marinara Sauce (page 90)

Prepare the spaghetti according to package directions.

Preheat the broiler. Line a baking sheet with foil and lightly coat the foil with olive oil.

In a large mixing bowl, combine the ground turkey, egg whites, bread crumbs, onion, zucchini, Parmesan, thyme, parsley, garlic, salt, and pepper. Mix together with your hands until evenly combined but not overworked; the resulting mixture should be supple. (Overmixing can cause the meat to break down, making it less conducive to forming meatballs.)

Using clean hands, roll the mixture into 12 balls of equal size. Place on the prepared baking sheet, spaced evenly apart. Broil 8 to 10 minutes, until the tops of the meatballs are golden brown.

Meanwhile, heat the Marinara Sauce in a large saucepan over medium-high heat.

Add the meatballs to the sauce and simmer until the meatballs are completely cooked through, about 15 minutes. Transfer to serving plates along with any extra sauce.

Marinara Sauce

YIELD: **About 4 cups, serving 4**

Make a double batch of this rich, hearty marinara sauce and freeze the extra for when you need a super-quick solution for dinner. It's a workhorse of a sauce, showing up in Turkey Meatballs here, along with Mini Chicken Parm Meatballs (page 86). It's a basic, must-have for pizza and whole wheat pasta. If you learn how to make only a handful of recipes, this should be one of them!

1 tablespoon olive oil

3 medium shallots, coarsely chopped

2 cloves garlic, minced

1 teaspoon sea salt, divided

½ teaspoon ground black pepper, divided

1 (28-ounce) can whole peeled tomatoes

1 cup quartered cherry tomatoes, divided

2 tablespoons fresh oregano leaves

1 tablespoon torn fresh basil leaves

Heat the olive oil in a large sauté pan over medium heat until the oil begins to ripple and shimmer. Add the shallots and sauté until beginning to soften, about 2 minutes. Add the garlic and stir for 1 minute. Season with ¼ teaspoon each of the salt and pepper, while continuing to stir.

Add the canned tomatoes, half of the cherry tomatoes, the oregano, basil, and remaining ³/₄ teaspoon salt and ¼ teaspoon pepper. Stir, crushing the whole tomatoes,* until the ingredients are evenly combined. Simmer over medium heat, uncovered, for 15 to 20 minutes.

Add the remaining cherry tomatoes and simmer for an additional 15 minutes. If preparing the sauce for Turkey Meatballs (page 89), add the meatballs along with the second batch of cherry tomatoes.

*TIP: Using canned whole tomatoes (as opposed to crushed) allows you to control the chunkiness of the sauce—for a more fluid, liquid marinara, crush the tomatoes thoroughly with your spoon as you stir, in order to release their juices; for a chunkier sauce, crush less. For the smoothest sauce, use crushed or pureed canned tomatoes and add all of the cherry tomatoes with the canned tomatoes.

Turkey Burgers

YIELD: **4 burgers**

Yes, your average turkey burger can be dry, but not these. When you add portobello mushrooms and egg whites, they are anything but. Flecked with chopped parsley, carrots, and onion, these super-moist patties need little more than a bun, but I top mine with a slice of cheese and avocado when I want something extra hearty.

1 portobello mushroom cap, stems removed, gills scraped and discarded, chopped

3 tablespoons packed coarsely chopped fresh flat-leaf parsley

2 tablespoons coarsely chopped carrot

1 tablespoon coarsely chopped sweet onion

1 pound lean ground turkey

2 large egg whites, lightly beaten

1 teaspoon Worcestershire sauce

¼ teaspoon sea salt

1 teaspoon ground black pepper

4 burger buns (100 percent whole grain), each sliced in half

4 slices reduced-fat Swiss cheese or light American cheese

Toppings of choice, such as avocado slices, lettuce leaves, tomato slices

In a food processor, combine the mushroom, parsley, carrots, and onion and process until extremely fine and well combined, 1 to 2 minutes.

In a large mixing bowl, combine the turkey, egg whites, Worcestershire sauce, salt, and pepper, doing so carefully and gently so as to avoid overworking the mixture. Add the vegetable mixture and mix until evenly distributed, again mixing lightly in order to prevent overworking.

(continued)

Divide the meat into 4 equal portions and roll each into a ball using the palms of your hands. Press into patties about 1½ inches thick and place on a plate. Make a small indentation in the middle of each to prevent the centers from expanding during cooking. Cover and refrigerate the patties for about 15 minutes to help the burgers maintain their shape during cooking.

Preheat the grill to medium or heat a grill pan over medium heat on the stovetop. Lightly coat the grate with canola oil. Grill the burgers, spaced several inches apart, for 4 to 5 minutes. Rotate a quarter turn and grill 4 to 5 minutes more. Flip the burgers and grill until thoroughly cooked through, 5 to 7 minutes longer.

To assemble, place a patty on the bottom half of each bun. Lay a slice of cheese on top, followed by your desired toppings. Top with the remaining buns and eat!

Turkey Tacos

YIELD: **6 tacos**

All of the traditional South-of-the-Border tastes—without the deep-fried factor—come together in these spiced-up taco cones. They're filled to the brim with some of my favorite healthful ingredients: caramelized onions, high-protein beans, and fresh cilantro.

½ cup diced sweet onion

2 tablespoons chopped cilantro

1 teaspoon whole cumin seeds

1 teaspoon garlic powder

¾ teaspoon chili powder

½ teaspoon paprika

½ teaspoon sea salt

Ground black pepper

1¼ pounds lean ground turkey

6 (6-inch) tortillas (100 percent whole grain)

1½ cups drained canned red kidney, white cannellini, and/or black beans

Toppings of choice, such as salsa, guacamole, reduced-fat sour cream, shredded reduced-fat Cheddar cheese

Preheat the oven to 400°F. Lightly coat a sauté pan with olive oil and set over medium heat. When the oil begins to shimmer, add the onion and sauté until tender and brown, 10 to 15 minutes.

Combine the cilantro, cumin, garlic powder, chili powder, paprika, salt, and pepper in a small bowl. If necessary, add more oil to the pan. Add the spice mixture and ground turkey. Cook, stirring with a wooden spoon or heatproof spatula to evenly distribute the spices throughout the meat while breaking up the turkey, until the turkey is completely browned and no longer pink, about 10 minutes.

While the turkey is cooking, place the tortillas on an ungreased baking sheet. Bake about 5 minutes, until lightly browned. Immediately fold each tortilla into a cone shape and place on a cone-shaped mold or serving dish (do so carefully as the tortillas are still hot). Setting the tortillas on the rim of a short plastic cup or glass will also produce the desired shape. Let cool for 5 to 10 minutes, then carefully remove the tortillas and set aside.

Gently fold the beans into the turkey mixture. Cook until the beans are heated through, 1 to 2 minutes more. Transfer to a heatproof plate or dish.

Place the toppings in individual small bowls. Spoon approximately ½ cup of the turkey mixture into each taco shell and serve with the toppings on the side.

Balsamic Pork Chops

YIELD: **4 servings**

When cooked down into a thick reduction, balsamic vinegar becomes a tangy syrup that makes an unrivaled coating for succulent pork chops. Pair with my Plum-Apple Chutney (page 144) for a simple, delicious meal.

2 tablespoons olive oil, divided

4 bone-in pork chops, about 6 to 8 ounces each

2 pounds sweet onions, thinly sliced

¼ cup plus 2 tablespoons balsamic vinegar

3 cups low-sodium chicken broth

1 tablespoon coarsely chopped fresh thyme

Heat 1 tablespoon of the oil in a large sauté pan over medium heat. Once the oil begins to shimmer, add the pork chops and sear 3 to 4 minutes per side. Remove to a plate.

Heat the remaining 1 tablespoon oil in the pan. Add the onions and season with salt and pepper. Cook, stirring, until tender, 10 to 15 minutes. Add the balsamic vinegar and cook, stirring occasionally, until reduced slightly, 2 to 3 minutes.

Return the pork chops to the pan and add the chicken broth and thyme. Cover, raise the heat to medium high, and simmer for 5 minutes. Uncover and cook until a meat thermometer inserted into the center of a pork chop registers 160°F, 2 to 3 minutes more. Serve with the onions and pan sauce. If desired, reduce and thicken the pan sauce (after removing the pork chops) by simmering an additional 10 minutes over medium-high heat.

Braised Pork Loin

Braising is one of the best cooking techniques for locking in flavor without adding extra fat. When you infuse the braising liquid with thyme and rosemary, the combination is irresistible. Here, oven-braising not only keeps the pork loin juicy, but it also produces a delicious gravy for drizzling on the sliced meat. This dish is guaranteed to be a family favorite.

½ cup low-sodium chicken broth

3 tablespoons olive oil

2 medium shallots, quartered

2 large cloves garlic, coarsely chopped

1 tablespoon plus 1 teaspoon fresh rosemary leaves

1 tablespoon plus 1 teaspoon fresh thyme leaves

½ teaspoon sea salt

½ teaspoon ground black pepper

1 pork loin, about 2½ pounds

3 or 4 fresh rosemary sprigs

3 or 4 fresh thyme sprigs

In the bowl of a food processor, combine the broth, oil, shallots, garlic, rosemary and thyme leaves, and salt and pepper and pulse until smooth.

Place the pork loin in a large roasting pan and pierce the meat all over with a fork. Pour the broth mixture over the pork loin. Submerge the rosemary and thyme sprigs in the liquid. Cover the pan with plastic wrap or aluminum foil and marinate 2 hours in the refrigerator.

Preheat the oven to 425°F. Uncover the roasting pan and transfer to the oven to bake 10 minutes. Reduce the heat to 400°F and bake an additional 35 to 40 minutes, until a meat thermometer inserted in the middle of the loin registers 160°F.

Cover the pan tightly with aluminum foil (to seal in heat) and let the pork rest at least 10 minutes (to prevent juices from escaping). Cut into thin slices and serve with the pan juices.

Pan-Seared Lamb Chops

YIELD: **2 to 3 servings (2 to 3 chops per serving)**

This recipe is super-easy—in just 3 steps, you can prepare a home-cooked version of an elegant restaurant standard and serve it proudly at your own dinner table. The simple, aromatic marinade permeates the meat with the pungent flavors of fresh herbs, garlic, and shallots. This versatile marinade is great on most any meat or poultry.

1 clove garlic, halved

1 medium shallot, quartered

6 tablespoons olive oil

1 tablespoon fresh marjoram

Leaves of 2 sprigs fresh rosemary

Leaves of 4 sprigs fresh thyme

2 tablespoons fresh flat-leaf parsley

⅛ teaspoon sea salt

Ground black pepper

6 bone-in lamb chops, about 3 to 4 ounces each

In a food processor, combine the garlic, shallot, and oil. Pulse until the texture is a nearly smooth, thick paste. Add the marjoram, rosemary, thyme, parsley, salt, and pepper and pulse until a thick paste has formed.

Place the lamb chops in a large baking dish. Spread the marinade over the lamb, cover with plastic wrap or aluminum foil, and marinate 4 hours in the refrigerator.

Heat a large sauté pan over medium heat. Place the chops in the pan (the oil in the marinade should be sufficient to prevent sticking, but add more to the pan if necessary). Cook 8 to 9 minutes per side for medium, until slightly pink in the middle.

Greek-Style Lamb Kabobs with Saffron Tzatziki

YIELD: **4 to 6 servings (2 to 3 skewers per serving)**

Food on a stick . . . who doesn't love that? Lamb kabobs are fun to grill up for a summertime backyard get-together, and they also make an ideal picnic option. The meat should marinate in the citrus and herb mixture for at least 1 hour, or ideally overnight, if time permits.

FOR THE MARINADE

¼ cup freshly squeezed orange juice

3 tablespoons olive oil

1 tablespoon low-sodium vegetable stock

¼ cup diced sweet onion

1 teaspoon grated lemon zest

2 tablespoons freshly squeezed lemon juice

2 tablespoons fresh thyme leaves

2 tablespoons fresh flat-leaf parsley

1 tablespoon minced garlic

½ teaspoon sea salt

FOR THE KABOBS

2 pounds lamb shoulder, cut into 1-inch chunks

1 red onion, cut into large chunks

2 yellow bell peppers, cut into large chunks

1 pound red grape tomatoes

1 pound button mushrooms, stems removed

Saffron Tzatziki (page 104)

To make the marinade, combine all the ingredients in a food processor and pulse until smooth.

Place the lamb in a large baking dish. Pour the marinade over and toss to coat. Cover with plastic wrap or aluminum foil and marinate at least 1 hour (or up to overnight) in the refrigerator.

Soak 12 wooden or bamboo skewers in water 20 to 30 minutes to prevent burning on the grill. When the lamb has marinated, thread the meat onto the skewers, alternating with chunks of the onion, pepper, tomato, and mushroom, as desired. Brush the vegetables with olive oil on all sides.

Heat the grill or grill pan to medium. Grill the skewers 5 minutes, flip using tongs, and grill 5 minutes more. Insert a meat thermometer in the thickest part of the lamb and be sure it reads 160°F for medium and the vegetables are well charred. Remove and serve with the Saffron Tzatziki.

Saffron Tzatziki

YIELD: **6 servings**

Tzatziki is a classic Greek dip consisting of thick, plain yogurt and cucumbers. It's delicious as is, but a hint of lemon zest adds tang and saffron imbues the creamy dip with a soft golden hue. I've lightened up traditional tzatziki by using nonfat Greek yogurt in place of the full-fat variety.

½ teaspoon saffron threads

2 teaspoons hot water

1 English cucumber, peeled, seeded, and finely grated

1 cup plain nonfat Greek yogurt

2 teaspoons olive oil

1 teaspoon honey

1 teaspoon grated lemon zest

2 teaspoons freshly squeezed lemon juice

3 tablespoons minced fresh flat-leaf parsley

2 tablespoons minced sweet onion

2 teaspoons minced garlic

¼ teaspoon sea salt

Ground black pepper

Lightly crush the saffron threads in a pestle. Add the hot water and let soak 15 minutes.

Drain the grated cucumber in a strainer or squeeze tightly in a paper towel to remove excess liquid.

In a bowl, combine the saffron threads and their liquid, the drained cucumber, yogurt, oil, honey, lemon zest and juice, parsley, onion, garlic, salt, and pepper. Whisk until well blended.

Serve alongside the Greek-Style Lamb Kabobs (page 102) or other favorite grilled dishes.

TIP: My Saffron Tzatziki also doubles as a kewl dip for fresh sliced vegetables or whole grain chips.

Grilled Skirt Steak

YIELD: **4 to 6 servings**

When my family wants to celebrate an exciting milestone, skirt steak is invariably on the menu. Inspired by the traditional restaurant preparation of Brazilian *churrascarias*, aka steak houses, the lean cut of meat is seasoned with a bold spice mixture that includes oregano, cumin, garlic powder, chili powder, and paprika. If you can't find skirt steak, flank steak is a great alternative.

2 tablespoons olive oil	1 teaspoon chili powder
1 tablespoon water	½ teaspoon paprika
2 tablespoons minced fresh oregano	½ teaspoon sea salt
2 teaspoons whole cumin seeds	⅛ teaspoon ground black pepper
2 teaspoons garlic powder	2 pounds skirt or flank steaks

In a small bowl, combine the oil, water, oregano, cumin, garlic powder, chili powder, paprika, salt, and pepper. Place the steaks in a large, wide baking dish and spread the spice mixture evenly over the top. Cover the dish with plastic wrap or aluminum foil and marinate 3 to 4 hours in the refrigerator.

Heat the grill or grill pan to medium high on the stovetop. Lightly coat the grates with olive oil. Add the steaks and grill 7 to 9 minutes, rotating 90 degrees (a quarter turn) halfway through. Flip the steaks and repeat, grilling the steaks until medium rare or medium well.*

Allow the steaks to rest at least 5 minutes (to prevent juices from escaping) before slicing on the diagonal and against the grain into thin strips.

*TIP: On my grill, medium high is about 400°F. Adjust times to correspond to the heat of your grill. Bear in mind these general time guidelines:

7 minutes per side, rotating halfway through = medium rare
9 minutes per side, rotating halfway through = medium well

Grilled Sliders

YIELD: 3 to 5 servings (2 to 3 sliders per serving)

If you're a through-and-through slider devotee like me, you know that they are hamburgers shrunken to appetizer size, which is a plus because then there are no excuses NOT to enjoy more than one! Swap out white buns for whole wheat, and you're guaranteed an added bonus of fiber. Sear, sizzle, and serve with Butternut Squash Fries (page 131).

½ cup diced sweet onion

3 tablespoons minced fresh flat-leaf parsley

1 tablespoon Dijon mustard

2 teaspoons minced garlic

½ teaspoon sea salt

½ teaspoon ground black pepper

1½ pounds 90 percent lean ground sirloin beef

3 tablespoons plus 1 teaspoon grated Cheddar cheese

10 whole wheat slider buns (if desired, hollow out extra bread)

Toppings of choice, such as lettuce, tomatoes, pickles, onions (optional)

In the bowl of a food processor, combine the onion, parsley, mustard, garlic, salt, and pepper and pulse to combine. Transfer to a large mixing bowl, add the ground beef, and stir until just incorporated.

Divide the meat into 10 equal portions and shape into balls. Make an indentation in the center of each ball with your thumb and fill with 1 teaspoon Cheddar. Cover the cheese with the meat and press down slightly to form a patty.

Preheat the grill to medium or heat a grill pan over medium heat on the stovetop. Lightly coat the grates with olive oil. Grill the sliders until browned and cooked through, 5 to 7 minutes per side. Place the patties on the buns, add toppings as desired, and serve.

Chapter 4
Pasta/Grains/Rice

THERE ARE AS MANY WAYS TO PREPARE PASTA, GRAINS, AND RICE AS THERE ARE COOKS, WHICH IS GOOD NEWS FOR ALL OF US.

When it comes to carbohydrates, the complex ones are the way to go. They energize you without causing your blood sugar to spike and later plummet, making you feel sluggish—what many of us experience as a crash. Simple carbohydrates (sweets, soft drinks, sugar, white flour) will do this every time and can eventually pack on extra pounds.

In this chapter, you'll discover some of my favorite recipes for **pasta, grains, and rice,** each one a delicious and flavorful source of whole grains and complex carbohydrates. When we think of whole grains, usually the first things that come to mind are brown rice, whole wheat pasta, and multigrain bread, right? But I've discovered options beyond these, and **farro and quinoa** are two of my favorites—they cook up much like rice, but offer different textures and flavors. Then there's **whole wheat pasta and brown rice,** both of which lend themselves to all manner of mix-ins: beef, chicken, pork, vegetables, spices, herbs, and nuts. My Kewl Quinoa (page 116) is a good example of the versatility of grains. A kaleidoscope of **colors, textures, and tastes,** it features citrusy kumquats; fresh, clean, green parsley; chewy dried cranberries and amber golden raisins; and crunchy pumpkin seeds and almonds. It's great for a sit-down lunch but is also perfect for packing to-go. Linguine with Clam Sauce (page 112) promises all the allure of the Italian restaurant classic without all the heft, while my Farro with Roasted Brussels Sprouts and Pine Nuts (page 119) is a revelation; who can resist crispy caramelized Brussels sprouts and lightly browned pine nuts in every bite?

Macadamia-Mint Couscous with Golden Raisins

YIELD: 4 servings

In minutes, serve up this satisfying bowl of couscous by simmering it in a mixture of hot water and broth. Couscous is a model of versatility—just stir in a mix of herbs, spices, nuts, dried fruits, or whatever you crave. I love the flavor and crunch of macadamia nuts, along with sweet golden raisins and fresh mint. This couscous combo is the ideal side dish for chicken, fish, or meat, or stands proudly all on its own.

1 (7.6-ounce) box whole wheat couscous

¾ cup low-sodium vegetable broth

¾ cup water

¾ cup macadamia nuts, chopped

½ cup golden raisins

¼ cup fresh mint leaves, coarsely chopped

2 tablespoons olive oil

¼ teaspoon sea salt

In a saucepan, combine the couscous, broth, and water and cook according to package instructions. Fluff with a fork and transfer to a large mixing bowl.

Stir in the nuts, raisins, mint, oil, and salt. Serve warm or chilled.

Linguine with Clam Sauce

YIELD: **4 to 6 servings**

I'm a huge fan of linguine with clam sauce! This recipe is a breakthrough—you won't find any butter or wine here, which are both ingredients in the classic dish. Neither is necessary when you can make a flavorful sauce with basil, parsley, and fresh lemon juice.

12 ounces whole grain linguine pasta

1 tablespoon olive oil

2 shallots, sliced into thin rings

1 clove garlic, minced

5 (5-ounce) cans minced clams, drained, with liquid reserved

2 tablespoons freshly squeezed lemon juice

¾ cup coarsely chopped fresh flat-leaf parsley, plus extra for garnish

1 tablespoon coarsely chopped fresh basil, plus extra for garnish

Bring a large pot of water to a boil over high heat. Add the linguine and cook according to package instructions until al dente, 7 to 10 minutes. Drain.

Meanwhile, heat the oil in a large skillet or sauté pan over medium heat. Once the oil begins to shimmer, add the shallots and sauté until lightly brown and caramelized, about 10 minutes. Add the garlic and cook 1 minute.

Add the reserved clam liquid, the lemon juice, parsley, and basil. Season with salt and pepper to taste. Raise the heat to medium high and simmer 15 minutes, until the sauce has reduced and thickened slightly. Stir in the clams and cook until heated through, 1 to 2 minutes.

Add the linguine and toss to coat thoroughly and distribute all the ingredients. Divide evenly among serving dishes and garnish with additional parsley and basil.

Shrimp Scampi

YIELD: **4 servings**

I'm breaking all the rules but maintaining all the definitive flavors of iconic shrimp scampi by cutting out the butter and oil. Instead, low-sodium seafood stock, shallots, and garlic make up the sauce. Serve this over your favorite whole grain pasta, shaped or long, from spaghetti to rotini, cooked according to package directions.

2 pounds medium shrimp, peeled and deveined

1 tablespoon olive oil

2 medium shallots, minced

2 cloves garlic, minced

¼ cup low-sodium seafood stock

½ teaspoon freshly grated lemon zest

2 tablespoons fresh lemon juice

2 tablespoons coarsely chopped fresh flat-leaf parsley

Cook the shrimp in a large pot of boiling water until opaque and slightly pink, about 5 minutes.

Heat the oil in a large skillet over medium-high heat. Add the shallots and cook until translucent, 2 to 3 minutes. Add the garlic and cook 1 minute, stirring occasionally.

Add the stock and lemon zest and juice. Simmer until the mixture has reduced slightly, 3 to 4 minutes. Add the parsley, season with salt and pepper, and cook 1 minute. Add the shrimp and toss to coat in the sauce, cooking 1 to 2 minutes to heat through. Serve and enjoy!

Pasta Primavera

YIELD: **4 servings**

Fresh veggies, such as zucchini and squash, are hallmarks of this pasta favorite, with lemon zest and a sprinkling of grated Parmesan heightening and brightening the flavors. I always use a distinctive shape of pasta, such as rotini, since the grooves are the best for trapping the vegetables and cheese.

2 medium zucchini, sliced into ½-inch-thick semicircles

2 medium yellow squash, sliced into ½-inch-thick semicircles

5 tablespoons olive oil, divided

1 tablespoon herbs de Provence (see tip on page 134)

2 teaspoons garlic powder

12 ounces whole grain rotini or other similarly shaped pasta

3 medium shallots, sliced into thin rings

3 medium cloves garlic, minced

8 ounces button mushrooms, stems removed and sliced

2 cups grape tomatoes (red, yellow, or combination), sliced in half

½ cup packed minced fresh flat-leaf parsley, plus extra for garnish

½ cup grated Parmesan cheese

Zest of 1 lemon

Preheat the oven to 450°F. Line a baking sheet with aluminum foil. In a large bowl, toss the zucchini and squash with 2 tablespoons of the olive oil, the herbs de Provence, and garlic powder and season with salt and pepper. Transfer to the baking sheet and bake 20 minutes, or until tender and slightly browned.

Bring a large pot of water to a boil over high heat. Add the pasta and cook according to package instructions until al dente. Drain and set aside in a large mixing bowl.

Heat the remaining 3 tablespoons oil in a large skillet over medium heat. Add the shallots and cook, stirring occasionally, 3 to 4 minutes. Add the garlic and cook 1 minute. Add the mushrooms and season with salt and pepper. Cook, stirring occasionally, until tender and browned, 10 minutes. Reduce the heat to low and stir in the tomatoes. Cook until their juices begin to release, 3 to 4 minutes. Add the zucchini/squash mixture and the mushroom/tomato mixture to the pasta, along with the parsley. Gently toss to combine. Serve warm, garnished with parsley, 2 tablespoons Parmesan cheese, and lemon zest.

Kewl Quinoa

YIELD: **6 to 8 servings**

This delicious salad is a show-stopping meal in itself, with a mix of sweetness thanks to soft cranberries and raisins, and crunch from the addition of pumpkin seeds and almonds. Quinoa, a grain that's mildly nutty in taste and light in texture, is a nutrition megastar because of its super-high protein content.

1½ cups dry prewashed organic quinoa

1½ cups low-sodium vegetable broth

1½ cups water

15 to 25 spears fresh asparagus (depending on thickness), tough ends removed, sliced into ½- to 1-inch pieces

½ cup fresh kumquats, sliced into thin rings and all seeds removed

¼ cup toasted unsalted pumpkin seeds (see tip on page 37)

¼ cup unsalted almonds, coarsely chopped

¼ cup minced fresh flat-leaf parsley

3 tablespoons dried cranberries

3 tablespoons golden raisins

Combine the quinoa, broth, and water in a medium saucepan over high heat. Bring to a boil, cover, and reduce the heat to low. Simmer for 10 to 15 minutes, until the quinoa has just absorbed all of the liquid and is tender. Remove from the heat, fluff with a fork, and transfer to a large, heatproof serving bowl. Set aside.

While the quinoa is cooking, coat a sauté pan with olive oil and set over medium heat. When the oil begins to shimmer, add the asparagus and season lightly with salt and pepper. Cook, stirring occasionally, until tender but still vibrantly green in color and not mushy in texture, 5 to 6 minutes.

To assemble the salad, add the asparagus, kumquats, pumpkin seeds, almonds, parsley, cranberries, and raisins to the cooked quinoa. Toss with a large spoon to combine. Drizzle in about 1 tablespoon olive oil and season with salt and pepper to taste. Toss once again to completely distribute. Serve warm or chilled.

Farro with Roasted Brussels Sprouts and Pine Nuts

YIELD: **4 to 6 servings**

Farro is a fabulous whole grain that cooks up just like pasta. With its intriguing, nutty flavor, it serves as a great foundation for any number of add-ins, from vegetables and nuts to dried fruits. Here, roasted Brussels sprouts and crispy toasted pine nuts team up for the perfect side dish. My tip: Soak the farro for 20 minutes before cooking; it mellows the mild tinge of bitterness that can be inherent to the grain.

1 cup uncooked farro, washed

2 cups low-sodium chicken broth

1 cup water

¾ teaspoon sea salt, divided

1 pound Brussels sprouts, stems removed and halved

3½ tablespoons olive oil, divided

½ teaspoon ground black pepper

1 large sweet onion, diced

½ cup pine nuts, toasted*

Preheat the oven to 400°F. Line a baking sheet with aluminum foil.

Place the farro in a bowl and add enough water to cover. Soak 20 minutes.

Drain the farro and transfer to a saucepan. Add the broth, water, and ¼ teaspoon of the salt and cook according to package instructions until the farro is al dente, 30 to 45 minutes. Drain and set aside.

Toss the Brussels sprouts, 2½ tablespoons of the oil, the remaining ½ teaspoon salt, and the pepper on the baking sheet. Bake 35 to 40 minutes, until fork-tender but crispy on the outside. Set aside to cool.

Meanwhile, heat the remaining 1 tablespoon oil in a saucepan over medium heat. Sauté the onions until tender and caramelized, 15 to 20 minutes.

In a large bowl, combine the cooked farro, Brussels sprouts, onions, and pine nuts. Serve family-style or transfer to individual bowls.

*TIP: To toast pine nuts (or any nut, for that matter), cook them in a dry sauté pan over medium heat for 3 to 4 minutes, or until golden brown and very fragrant, stirring the nuts or shaking the pan occasionally. They toast really quickly, so be sure to keep an eye locked on!

Shanghai Vegetable Fried Rice

YIELD: **4 servings**

What's the Chinese phrase for "delicious"? Fried rice! My take on it (actually, not "fried" per se, but stir-fried in a traditional wok) is loaded with crisp-tender veggies and assertive Asian flavors. You'll never want to order takeout again. Added bonus: The delicious aroma of ginger and garlic will permeate your kitchen.

1 tablespoon canola oil

2 tablespoons minced fresh ginger

2 tablespoons minced garlic

3 large eggs

1 cup drained canned bamboo shoots

1 cup bean sprouts

1 cup thinly sliced bok choy, white parts only

1 cup broccoli florets

1 cup shredded carrots

2 cups cooked whole grain brown rice

¾ cup thinly sliced scallions, white and green parts, plus extra for garnish

3 tablespoons soy sauce

3 tablespoons hoisin sauce

3 tablespoons water

Sesame seeds, for garnish

Heat the oil in a wok (or similarly large wide pan with high, curved sides) over high heat or in an electric wok. Add the ginger and garlic and cook, stirring often, about 2 minutes. Add the eggs and scramble, breaking them into small chunks with a spatula, 3 to 4 minutes.

Add the bamboo shoots, bean sprouts, bok choy, broccoli, and carrots. Season with salt and pepper. Cook, stirring occasionally, until tender, 5 to 7 minutes.

Add the rice, scallions, soy sauce, hoisin sauce, and water. Reduce the heat to medium and cook, stirring occasionally, 2 to 3 minutes.

Divide evenly among 4 bowls and garnish with sesame seeds and extra scallions.

Chapter 5
Sides

DON'T TAKE THE WORD "SIDE" LITERALLY.

The dishes in this chapter are worthy of the center of the plate. I love a versatile side dish, one that is right at home either in the middle or off to the edge of the plate. Side dishes not only round out a meal and provide an opportunity to work seasonal vegetables into your diet, but a combination of them can actually make a meal. For instance, when I'm a little tired of the same-old, same-old, I turn to this chapter to make my recipe for yummy Veggie Dumplings (page 139), which are a perfect companion to Grilled Vegetable Stackers (page 136). These two recipes are not only simpatico, but they comprise a wonderful vegetable-based meal, which is never a bad thing. Or, dip into the salads chapter (page 25) to expand your options. A combination of three sides inevitably makes for a colorful plate—one of the keys to healthy eating.

Of course, the ideal side dish is one that we can eat without regret. Sadly, one of my favorites—French fries—does not fall into this category. But rather than giving them up, I simply turned to a more colorful substitute, butternut squash, cut it into spears and roasted. No more deep frying! In fact, another one of my favorite all-sides meals is Butternut Squash Fries (yum) (page 131), Caramelized Mushrooms and Onions (page 141) and Stuffed Artichokes (page 129), made healthier with a lighter stuffing. I put the artichoke in the center of the plate and arrange the other two dishes around it. The artichokes also make a great dinner companion with Chinese-style steamed Vegetable Dumplings (page 139), on their own, make the perfect lunch. I've served up the artichokes and dumplings at parties and they've been a huge hit. Just double the ingredients to make them for a crowd!

Of course, there are very specific occasions when side dishes should play their original role. The holidays wouldn't be the same without a spread of sides, but the offerings aren't always the healthiest. Unfortunately, they're usually loaded with lots of heavy cream, butter, oil, salt, and sugar—ingredients that can take the "festive" right out of the festivities. Luckily, there's no need to forego your favorites, because this chapter is full of dishes that you will be proud to offer on your celebration table. For instance, there are the Roasted Vegetable Medley (page 132) and Roasted Fingerling Potatoes (page 134)—the perfect swap-out for mashed potatoes. My recipe for Roasted Rainbow Candied Carrots (page 126), raises this humble vegetable to a holiday-worthy dish. And what turkey dinner would be complete without ruby red cranberry sauce? I've come up with delicious alternatives to that sugar-laden classic in Plum-Apple Chutney (page 144) and Apple-Pear Compote with Vanilla Bean (page 142). Whether the farmstands are groaning with fresh produce, you're planning your next holiday menu, or simply looking to change up the center of your plate, flip through this chapter to find some delicious answers.

Roasted Rainbow Candied Carrots

YIELD: 4 servings

Tossed with maple syrup, seasoned with cinnamon, and roasted, sweet carrots get just a tad sweeter! This gorgeous dish is a staple on my family's Thanksgiving table, but it's worth making whenever the piles of multicolored carrots start to show up at the farmers' market or your favorite grocery store.

2½ tablespoons maple syrup

1½ tablespoons canola oil

1¼ teaspoons ground cinnamon

⅛ teaspoon sea salt

2 pounds multicolored carrots (orange, yellow, purple), peeled
(if using mini carrots, leave stems on)

Preheat the oven to 375°F. Line a baking sheet with aluminum foil.

In a small bowl, combine the syrup, oil, cinnamon, and salt. Toss with the carrots in a large bowl until evenly coated.

Spread on the baking sheet in a single layer. Bake 35 minutes or until fork-tender.

Stuffed Artichokes

YIELD: 4 servings

Artichokes are among the most fun vegetables to eat. Even better, they're packed with antioxidants and are a great source of fiber. Peel back the leaves one by one and slide them between your teeth to enjoy their smooth, earthy flesh. The top prize is the heart, a tender nugget at the core of the artichoke. Here, I've tucked a crumbly herb and bread crumb stuffing spiked with lemon and Parmesan in between each leaf. Make these for a party—your guests will never forget them!

4 large artichokes

1 lemon, halved

2 tablespoons olive oil

1 medium sweet onion, diced

3 medium cloves garlic, minced

2 cups whole grain bread crumbs (coarsely ground in food processor from fresh or day-old crusty bread)

¼ cup coarsely chopped fresh flat-leaf parsley

¼ cup coarsely chopped fresh oregano leaves

1 teaspoon grated lemon zest

½ teaspoon sea salt

¼ teaspoon ground black pepper

¾ cup grated Parmesan cheese, divided

2 cups boiling water

Olive oil cooking spray

Slice off the artichoke stems and tops using a serrated knife and remove any rough leaves or sharp leaf tips using scissors or kitchen shears. Scoop out and discard the interior chokes and the spiny parts. Rub the lemon halves over the sliced portions and outer exterior edges of the artichokes to prevent browning.

Preheat the oven to 425°F. Heat the oil in a sauté pan over medium heat. Sauté the onions until just translucent, 5 to 8 minutes. Add the garlic and cook, stirring often, 2 minutes.

(continued)

Add the bread crumbs and toast, stirring occasionally, until crispy, about 5 minutes. Add the parsley, oregano, and lemon zest. Cook 1 to 2 minutes to heat through. Add the salt and pepper and stir to combine.

Transfer the bread crumb mixture to a medium bowl and mix in $1/2$ cup plus 2 tablespoons of the Parmesan cheese. Scoop the mixture evenly into the cavities of the 4 artichokes and between the leaves. Place the artichokes, stuffing side up, in a 2-quart baking dish, and pour the boiling water around them.

Coat a long sheet (2 if necessary) of aluminum foil with olive oil cooking spray. Place the foil over the artichokes and wrap the dish tightly, making a tent over the entire baking dish. Bake 45 to 50 minutes, until the artichokes are very tender.

Remove the foil tent and sprinkle the remaining 2 tablespoons Parmesan evenly over the artichokes. Change the oven setting to broil and broil the artichokes for 3 minutes, or until they are golden brown on top.

Butternut Squash Fries

YIELD: 4 to 6 servings

It's no secret that French fries are deep-fried in tons of fat, but the truth is, you can satisfy a craving for the crispy, salty side dish in a much healthier way. I opt for nutrient-rich butternut squash fries and roll them in cornflakes seasoned with dried herbs to create a super-crunchy coating. (See photo on page 107.)

2 large egg whites, lightly beaten

1 cup unsweetened cornflakes cereal, crushed

2 teaspoons garlic powder

1 teaspoon dried marjoram

1 teaspoon dried oregano

1 teaspoon dried savory

1 teaspoon dried thyme

¾ teaspoon sea salt

¼ teaspoon ground black pepper

2 small butternut squash, peeled, seeded, and sliced into matchsticks

Preheat the oven to 425°F. Line a baking sheet with aluminum foil and lightly coat with olive oil.

Place the egg whites in a bowl. In a wide baking dish, combine the crushed cornflakes, garlic powder, marjoram, oregano, savory, thyme, salt, and pepper.

Using tongs, dip the squash fries into the egg whites until coated. Transfer to the cornflakes mixture and coat on all sides. Place on the baking sheet in a single, even layer.

Bake 40 to 45 minutes, until the inside is fork-tender and the outside is crispy. Serve immediately.

Roasted Vegetable Medley

YIELD: 4 servings

Roasting is one of my favorite (and one of the healthiest) ways to cook vegetables. The process of roasting concentrates the natural sugars in the veggies and gives them a crisp, sweet exterior. I love herbes de Provence, but you can experiment with whatever combination of dried herbs you like.

8 ounces mini carrots, tops left on

8 ounces baby summer squash

8 ounces baby zucchini

2 tablespoons olive oil

2 tablespoons herbes de Provence (see tip on page 134)

2 teaspoons garlic powder

½ teaspoon sea salt

½ teaspoon ground black pepper

Preheat the oven to 400°F. Line a large baking sheet with aluminum foil.

Combine the carrots, squash, zucchini, oil, herbes de Provence, garlic powder, salt, and pepper in a large bowl and toss to coat evenly.

Spread the vegetables* on the prepared baking sheet in a single layer and bake 20 minutes. Stir, return to the oven, and bake 20 minutes. Stir again and bake 10 minutes more, until the vegetables are fork-tender. Serve immediately, while warm.

*TIP: This recipe features mini vegetables, which are ideal for roasting whole. If you can't track down the mini variety, no worries! Simply slice regular vegetables into chunks of the same size to ensure that their roasting time will be the same and that they all cook evenly throughout.

Roasted Fingerling Potatoes

YIELD: 6 to 8 servings

Here is the kewlest mix of mini potatoes and onions ever. I love to use a mixture of colors for the potatoes—they're available in red, yellow, and purple at farmers' markets and gourmet food shops. The trick here is to toss them in enough olive oil to coat them thoroughly and to season them well.

3 pounds fingerling potatoes (a mixture of red, yellow, and purple)

1 pound red and white pearl onions

¼ cup olive oil

2 teaspoons herbes de Provence*

1 teaspoon garlic powder

1 teaspoon sea salt

½ teaspoon ground black pepper

Preheat the oven to 350°F. Coat a 9- by 13-inch baking sheet with olive oil.

In a large mixing bowl, toss the potatoes and onions with oil. Add the herbes de Provence, garlic powder, salt, and pepper and toss until the seasonings are evenly distributed. Spread the potatoes and onions onto the baking sheet in a single layer.

Bake 60 to 75 minutes, stirring once halfway through, until the potatoes and onions are fork-tender. Transfer to a large dish or bowl and serve warm.

*TIP: Don't let the French name intimidate you! Herbes de Provence is a delicious combination of dried herbs (thyme, marjoram, savory, rosemary, basil, and more) that goes very well with potatoes and onions. (You may also wish to try the recipe on page 132.)

Grilled Vegetable Stackers

YIELD: 4 servings

Essentially a veggie sandwich minus the bread, these colorful towers of grilled vegetables drizzled with a sweet balsamic glaze are very forgiving. Use whatever vegetables are in season; just follow the method for grilling, stacking, and drizzling.

1 cup balsamic vinegar

4 large, round, thick slices of eggplant

2 red bell peppers, halved, and stems, seeds, and veins removed

2 yellow bell peppers, halved, and stems, seeds, and veins removed

4 large portobello mushroom caps, stems and gills removed

4 thick slices of a large sweet onion

4 tablespoons shredded reduced-fat mozzarella cheese

Bring the vinegar to a boil in a saucepan over high heat and immediately reduce the heat to low. Cook, stirring occasionally, until thickened and syrupy, 30 to 35 minutes. Set aside.

Preheat the grill to medium-high or heat a grill pan over medium-high on the stovetop. Lightly coat the grate with olive oil. Lightly brush the eggplant slices, bell pepper halves, mushroom caps, and onion slices with olive oil and season on both sides with garlic powder, salt, and pepper. Working in batches, grill the vegetables until just tender.

Stack the vegetables on 4 serving plates to form tall towers, starting with a mushroom cap, and followed by an eggplant slice, onion slice, yellow pepper, and red pepper.

Sprinkle 1 tablespoon mozzarella on the top of each tower, then drizzle each with a tablespoon of balsamic glaze.*

*TIP: Take a page from restaurant chefs and use this awesome trick to drizzle the balsamic glaze over the towers: Pour the glaze into a squeezable squirt bottle and squeeze decorative patterns on the vegetable stacks and plates.

Vegetable Dumplings with Lemongrass Dipping Sauce

YIELD: 6 servings (about 6 dumplings per serving)

These Vegetable Dumplings are my take on classic Dim Sum. I had so much fun creating this recipe. It features envelope-shaped dumplings made from wonton wrappers, which become translucent when steamed—a great cooking method that requires no fat. Once cooked, the vibrant colors of the vegetables show through ever so slightly. Mini masterpieces!

¼ cup low-sodium chicken broth

2 tablespoons reduced-sodium soy sauce

2 tablespoons sesame seeds

1 tablespoon coarsely chopped fresh ginger

2 cloves garlic, coarsely chopped

2 large egg whites

½ teaspoon sea salt

¼ teaspoon ground black pepper

½ cup grated carrots

½ cup finely grated red Napa cabbage

½ cup shelled edamame

½ cup diced water chestnuts

1 red or yellow bell pepper, diced

¼ cup cilantro leaves

1 package miniature (2-inch) square wonton wrappers (35 total)

Lemongrass Dipping Sauce (page 140)

In a food processor, pulse the broth, soy sauce, sesame seeds, ginger, garlic, egg whites, salt, and pepper until smooth.

To make the filling, in a mixing bowl, combine the carrots, cabbage, edamame, water chestnuts, bell pepper, and cilantro. Pour about half of the mixture from the food processor over the vegetables.

Place 1 wrapper on a work surface and lightly brush the edges with water. Spoon 1½ teaspoons of the filling in the center, draining excess liquid before adding to the wrapper. Fold 1 corner of the wrapper over the mixture, followed by the opposite corner, to create an egg roll shape that is open at the sides. Fold the remaining 2 corners over each other and press

(continued)

down firmly to seal the wrapper tightly. Repeat with the remaining wrappers and filling to make a total of 35 dumplings.

Fill a large sauté pan with high sides with about $\frac{1}{2}$ inch of water. Set over medium heat and bring to a simmer. Place the dumplings in a single layer in a metal or bamboo steamer lined with parchment paper and place the steamer in the pan. Cover and steam the dumplings about 12 minutes, until the wrappers are glossy and slightly translucent and the vegetables are tender. Carefully remove the dumplings to a plate. Repeat to steam all the dumplings, refilling the pan with water as necessary. Serve with the dipping sauce.

Lemongrass Dipping Sauce

YIELD: Approximately 1 cup

1 cup cilantro leaves

$\frac{1}{2}$ cup thinly sliced stalks lemongrass

$\frac{1}{4}$ cup reduced-sodium soy sauce

$\frac{1}{4}$ cup low-sodium chicken broth

$\frac{1}{4}$ cup water

In a food processor, pulse all the ingredients until smooth. Serve alongside the dumplings for dipping.

Caramelized Mushrooms and Onions

YIELD: **4 servings**

This is inspired by the classic steak house offering, typically served alongside a perfectly grilled piece of meat. But I prefer to spoon the delicious mix into a split baked potato or on top of Grilled Sliders (page 106), or perhaps just serve it with a variety of other side dishes to make up a vegetarian meal.

2 tablespoons olive oil

3 large sweet yellow onions, cut into ¼-inch-thick slices

8 cups white button mushrooms, stems removed, thinly sliced

Heat the oil in a large sauté pan over medium heat. Add the onions and cook, stirring occasionally, about 10 minutes. Add the mushrooms and season with the salt and pepper. Cook, stirring occasionally, until the liquid has reduced and the onions and mushrooms have caramelized, 25 to 30 minutes. Serve immediately, while still warm.

Apple-Pear Compote with Vanilla Bean

YIELD: 6 to 8 servings

This warm, sweet compote is perfect for breakfast or a festive holiday brunch. Loaded with fresh fruit and myriad wintertime flavors like cinnamon and allspice, you'll love using it as an alternative to maple syrup on waffles or pancakes. It also makes a delicious accompaniment to roast chicken.

2 pounds Bosc pears, peeled, quartered, and cored

2 pounds sweet red apples, peeled, quartered, and cored

½ cup freshly steeped decaffeinated vanilla-flavored black tea

⅓ cup pure maple syrup

Zest of ½ medium orange

¼ cup freshly squeezed orange juice

1 teaspoon ground cinnamon

½ teaspoon ground allspice

¼ teaspoon sea salt

2 vanilla beans, split open and seeds scraped

Combine the pears, apples, tea, maple syrup, orange zest and juice, cinnamon, allspice, salt, and vanilla bean seeds in a large Dutch oven or stockpot and stir to combine. Cover and bring to a boil over high heat. Reduce the heat to medium and simmer, covered, until the apples and pears are fork-tender, 30 to 40 minutes. Uncover and continue to cook for 5 minutes, stirring often, until the liquid has reduced to a thick syrup.

Using a potato masher or the edge of a wooden or metal spoon, mash the apples and pears just until chunky, if desired, or continue to mash to a smooth, uniform puree.

Serve hot or cold. Store any leftovers in an airtight container in the refrigerator.

Plum-Apple Chutney

YIELD: 4 to 6 servings

To boil it down (no pun intended!): This simple fruit compote of apples, plums, sugar, and spices is as versatile a condiment as it gets. It's the perfect accompaniment to my Balsamic Pork Chops (page 96) and just about any meat or poultry you cook in the fall months.

2 pounds Fuji apples, cored and quartered (skins left on)

2 pounds red plums, pitted and chopped into 2-inch chunks (skins left on)

¾ cup water

¼ cup unsweetened apple juice

¼ cup plus 2 tablespoons raw sugar

2 teaspoons ground cinnamon

2 teaspoons vanilla extract

Combine the apples, plums, water, apple juice, sugar, and cinnamon in a large pot. Cover and bring to a boil over medium heat. Reduce the heat to low and simmer until the fruits are fork-tender, about 40 minutes.

Stir in the vanilla extract and simmer 1 minute. Allow to cool slightly. Serve warm or chilled.

Chapter ⑥
Sweet and Savory Snacks

SNACK TIME OFTEN GETS A BAD RAP AND I'M PRETTY SURE I KNOW WHY. My memories of snacking begin in preschool when cupcakes, potato chips, and chocolate were mainstays. Looking back, I realize that the idea of staving off hunger was an excuse for dessert, with sugar being the main ingredient. Nutrition and snack time were two concepts that, for the longest time, I didn't put together. Now, of course, I distinguish between snacks and treats, and the results are undeniable. But previously, snack time always meant a few non-nutritious treats and evolved from a holdover to a meal to a multicourse feast in itself. My poor snacking pattern began after school (if it hadn't already been initiated there) and continued after dinner. Before I knew it, the runaway snack train had veered completely off the rails.

When I decided to take a good, hard look at my eating habits, I knew snacking was the place to start. First, I had to understand why I was craving snacks so often. For instance, on a normal school day, I would eat breakfast between 6:30 and 7:00 a.m., with lunch not until noon. My stomach wasn't built to stay fueled for such a long stretch of time! Also, with lunch at noon and dinner at roughly 6:00 p.m., there was another lengthy time in which hunger was constantly creeping up. I noticed that I felt ravenous, tired, and irritable by the next mealtime.

Wanting to be fueled and sharp for those midmorning and midafternoon hours, I figured out that choosing fuel-rich snacks would keep me energized and focused. I began to think of snack time as the bridge between breakfast and lunch and lunch and dinner. In bridging the gap between meals, I started to develop a smart snacking strategy.

Throughout all my research, what I learned about snacking flows back to the basics. Sure, a sugary treat might provide momentary bliss and, without a doubt, it's fun to munch on. But it won't keep your blood sugar in balance or fuel your body properly. It will cause your sugar to spike and ultimately, you'll be more tired and irritable than you were before you indulged!

Smart snacking means limiting them to twice a day and choosing "snacks with benefits," as I like to refer to them. By benefits, I mean selections that include a blend of protein, fiber, complex carbohydrates, and healthy fats (monounsaturated, that is). Snacks with these ingredients are truly satisfying—they don't trick your body into thinking you're happy, and then let you down.

This chapter features many of my favorite snack recipes; they're not only delicious, but also practical. While I often snack on the go, I never rely on store-bought snacks no matter how time-pressed I am. For instance, granola or energy bars are super-popular at most markets and fast-food spots, but most are loaded with sugar, and some contain unhealthy fats. My Kewl Krunch Bars (page 155) are a healthy homemade take on these popular treats. I usually double-batch the simple recipe, wrap the bars tightly in aluminum foil, slide them into a resealable plastic bag, and freeze. When I need one, whether it's for an on-the-run breakfast, excursion in the air or on the road, or just a satiating treat, it's ready to go.

It's essential to find snack options that are tasty and satisfying. Some people prefer savory snacks, others love sweet ones. I've rounded out the offerings to cover both desires. What's more, some of them—Fig and Apple Bars (page 150), Kewl Krunch Bars (page 155), Homemade Granola (page 156), and Lemon, Raspberry, and Poppy Seed Muffins (page 161)—can stand in for breakfast if you're really time-pressed in the morning.

If you like crunchy snacks, check out the three flavors of popcorn options. If you like to dip, you'll love my fondue-style Triple-Chocolate Almond Butter (page 151). And, if you prefer homemade baked goods, try my Apple Spice Cakes (page 157) or Dark-Chocolate Banana Marble Bread (page 158). Both are fruit-based and totally satisfying. Any one of these can be packed to snack on the go—and is far more satisfying than the packaged snacks loaded with processed ingredients, artificial flavors, and bad fats. With my yummy snacks on your side, moving over to the healthy side will be a snap.
Happy snacking!

Fig and Apple Bars

YIELD: **16 bars**

This recipe was inspired by the classic fig-filled cookies we all grew up with. But unlike those packaged treats, these are made with a combination of whole wheat and white flour and contain far less sugar. They make excellent portable snacks, perfect for sliding into your coat pocket.

1½ cups whole wheat flour

2 cups all-purpose flour

2 teaspoons baking powder

½ teaspoon salt

2 large eggs

1 cup unsweetened applesauce

½ cup raw sugar

¼ cup canola oil

¼ cup plus 2 tablespoons nonfat plain Greek yogurt

2 teaspoons pure vanilla extract

8 ounces whole figs, coarsely chopped

5 ounces dried apples

¼ cup water

1 tablespoon honey

2 teaspoons lemon juice

1 teaspoon ground cinnamon

In a large bowl, combine the whole wheat flour, all-purpose flour, baking powder, and salt.

In a separate bowl, combine the eggs, applesauce, sugar, oil, yogurt, and vanilla extract. Blend until completely combined.

Gently fold the wet ingredients into the dry until the dough is evenly mixed. Divide into 2 equal portions, wrap each separately in plastic wrap, and refrigerate for 40 minutes, until chilled.

Preheat the oven to 375°F. Lightly coat a 9-inch square baking pan with canola oil.

In a food processor, pulse the figs and dried apples until fine. Add the water, honey, lemon juice, and cinnamon. Pulse until just combined.

Pat 1 portion of dough into the bottom of the prepared pan. Top with the fig mixture, making an even layer. Top with the remaining portion of dough, spreading evenly. Bake for 25 to 27 minutes, until golden brown. Let cool 10 minutes before cutting into 16 squares.

Triple-Chocolate Almond Butter

YIELD: ¾ to 1 cup, serving 4

My version of hazelnut spread is as rich and creamy as the jarred kind without the unhealthy palm oil. Spread on slices of fresh, potassium-rich bananas or apple wedges for the perfect afternoon pick-me-up.

½ cup creamy almond butter

2 tablespoons unsweetened natural cocoa powder

2 tablespoons dark chocolate chips

2 tablespoons honey

2 teaspoons chocolate extract

In a bowl, combine the almond butter, cocoa powder, chocolate chips, honey, and chocolate extract to form a thick, creamy butter.

Serve with apple wedges, pear slices, and banana slices.

Biscotti Bites

YIELD: **24 to 30 biscotti**

These traditional Italian cookies are among my favorites. I discovered them when I was in Italy and just knew that I had to create my own version. Literally translated, *biscotti* means "twice cooked," which accounts for their super-crunchy texture. They are traditionally dipped into coffee or tea, but you can dip them into any hot drink and enjoy their citrusy, nutty flavor.

2 large eggs	1 cup all-purpose flour
2 large egg whites	1 cup almond flour
2 tablespoons creamy almond butter	¼ cup raw sugar
1½ teaspoons almond extract	2 teaspoons baking powder
1 teaspoon grated orange zest	½ cup almonds, coarsely chopped

Preheat the oven to 300°F. Line a baking sheet with parchment paper.

In the bowl of a standing mixer fitted with the paddle attachment (or using a hand mixer), beat the eggs, egg whites, almond butter, almond extract, and orange zest until smooth.

In a separate bowl, whisk together the all-purpose flour, almond flour, sugar, and baking powder.

With the mixer on low, gradually incorporate the dry ingredients into the wet in 3 even additions, until just combined. Stir in the chopped almonds.

Divide the batter into 2 equal portions and roll each into a 4- by 12-inch log. Place on the baking sheet, spacing several inches apart and pressing down to flatten the logs slightly. Bake for 1 hour.

Slice each log crosswise into approximately ½-inch-thick slices. Arrange, cut side up, on the baking sheet. Reduce the heat to 275°F and bake 30 minutes. Turn the biscotti over and bake 15 minutes, or until golden. Let cool and harden before serving.

Kewl Krunch Bars

YIELD: **20 bars**

Making your own energy bars is the best way to control what ingredients go into your snacks. Teeming with a variety of dried fruits and nuts, as well as oats, whole wheat flour, and wheat germ, these bars are chock-full of healthy, filling fiber and delicious flavors. Pack in your backpack, briefcase, or back pocket for a midday energy boost! I always bake a double batch and freeze one. This makes it easy to reach for a bar before I get on a plane or go out on the road.

2 cups instant or quick-cooking oatmeal

1 cup whole wheat flour

¾ cup raw sugar

½ cup wheat germ

½ teaspoon ground cinnamon

½ teaspoon sea salt

½ cup honey

¼ cup unsweetened applesauce

¼ cup canola oil

2 large egg whites

¾ cup coarsely chopped dried cherries

½ cup coarsely chopped dried apricots

¼ cup coarsely chopped almonds

¼ cup coarsely chopped walnuts

Preheat the oven to 350°F. Lightly coat a 9- by 13-inch rimmed baking sheet with canola oil.

In a large bowl, combine the oats, flour, sugar, wheat germ, cinnamon, and salt. Stir to thoroughly combine.

In a smaller bowl, combine the honey, applesauce, oil, and egg whites.

Pour the wet ingredients into the dry and stir to form a rich, thick batter. Add the cherries, apricots, almonds, and walnuts and stir until completely distributed.

Press the batter into the baking sheet, until it completely covers the sheet in a smooth and even layer. Bake for 25 to 30 minutes, until cooked through.

Let cool completely before cutting into 20 rectangular bars. (Make 1 cut lengthwise and then 10 horizontal cuts to create 20 bars.)

Homemade Granola

YIELD: Approximately 4 cups granola, serving 8

Homemade granola can be just the ticket when you need a quick refueling. It's great on its own, but makes a great topping to a yogurt parfait, too. Store in an airtight container to maintain optimal freshness.

2½ cups rolled oats

2 teaspoons ground cinnamon

½ teaspoon sea salt

¼ cup honey

¼ cup raw sugar

3 tablespoons canola oil

2 tablespoons unsweetened applesauce

2 teaspoons pure vanilla extract

½ cup sunflower seeds

⅓ cup dried cranberries

⅓ cup dried blueberries

Preheat the oven to 325°F. Line a baking sheet with parchment paper.

In a large bowl, combine the oats, cinnamon, and salt. In a medium bowl, combine the honey, sugar, oil, applesauce, and vanilla extract. Add the wet ingredients to the dry and mix well.

Spread the mixture evenly on the prepared baking sheet and bake for 12 minutes. Stir with a spatula, return to the oven, and bake 12 minutes, or until golden. Let cool 5 minutes.

In a medium bowl, combine the sunflower seeds, cranberries, and blueberries. Stir into the granola and then return to the oven to bake 5 minutes. Remove, stir to break up any chunks, and allow to cool. Serve warm or store in airtight containers.

Apple Spice Cakes

YIELD: 8 mini Bundt cakes (or 1 large Bundt cake)

I serve these mini Bundt cakes, fragrant of allspice and cinnamon, at holiday time and also present them as gifts. I like to wrap them in colorful plastic wrap and tie them with ribbon for friends and teachers.

1½ cups all-purpose flour

½ cup whole wheat flour

1¼ cups raw sugar

2 teaspoons ground cinnamon

1 teaspoon ground allspice

½ teaspoon freshly grated nutmeg

1 teaspoon baking soda

1 teaspoon baking powder

¼ teaspoon sea salt

½ cup canola oil

½ cup unsweetened applesauce

2 large eggs

1 large egg white

1 teaspoon pure vanilla extract

2 large sweet red apples, peeled, cored, and chopped

Confectioners' sugar, for dusting

Preheat the oven to 350°F. Lightly coat 8 molds of a mini Bundt cake pan with canola oil.

In a large mixing bowl, whisk together the all-purpose flour, whole wheat flour, sugar, cinnamon, allspice, nutmeg, baking soda, baking powder, and salt.

In a separate bowl, beat together the oil, applesauce, eggs, egg white, and vanilla extract.

Pour the wet ingredients into the dry and mix until just combined. Stir in the apples until distributed.

Divide the batter evenly among the 8 prepared cups of the cake pan. Bake for approximately 40 minutes. (Or spoon into a greased large Bundt pan and bake for 1 hour.) To check for doneness, insert a toothpick into the center of 1 cake (or the large cake). If the pick comes out clean, the cakes are done. If any wet or uncooked batter remains on the toothpick, continue to bake in 5-minute increments until baked through.

Allow the cakes to cool completely, 15 to 20 minutes, before removing from their molds and inverting onto plates to serve. Use a fine mesh strainer to evenly dust each cake with a fine layer of confectioners' sugar.

Dark-Chocolate Banana Marble Bread

YIELD: 1 cake, approximately 10 slices

A mosaic of smooth dark chocolate and fresh sweet bananas, this special bread is so light and airy that it bakes up like a soufflé! I've replaced butter with a healthier alternative: peanut butter. A baker's confession: While I have included this recipe in the snack chapter, I have been known to indulge in it for breakfast!

1 cup raw sugar

3 tablespoons unsweetened organic peanut butter

1 tablespoon canola oil

1½ cups mashed very ripe bananas

⅓ cup nonfat plain Greek yogurt

2 large eggs

1 large egg white

1 teaspoon pure vanilla extract

1¼ cups all-purpose flour

¾ cup oat flour

½ teaspoon baking powder

½ teaspoon baking soda

¼ teaspoon sea salt

¾ cup dark chocolate chips

Preheat the oven to 350°F. Lightly coat a 8½- by 4½-inch loaf pan with canola oil.

In the bowl of a standing mixer fitted with the paddle attachment or using a handheld mixer, cream together the sugar, peanut butter, and oil. Add the bananas and yogurt and beat until smooth. Add the eggs and egg white, one at a time, mixing constantly on medium speed, until combined. Stir in the vanilla extract.

In a separate bowl, whisk together the all-purpose flour, oat flour, baking powder, baking soda, and salt. Using a wooden spoon, gradually mix the dry ingredients into the wet in 3 to 4 additions until just combined.

Microwave the chocolate in a medium heatproof bowl until melted and completely smooth. Stir about half of the batter into the melted chocolate until evenly combined.

Spoon the plain and chocolate batters into the prepared loaf pan, alternating spoonfuls of each. Gently swirl the batters with a knife. Bake 1 hour, or until a toothpick inserted into the center of the bread comes out clean.

Lemon, Raspberry, and Poppy Seed Muffins

YIELD: 12 muffins

These muffins are a spectacular snack with a moist interior and a slightly crunchy crown, perfect for all muffin eaters: those who love the tops and others who prefer the soft inside.

2 cups oat flour

¾ cup raw sugar

1½ teaspoons baking powder

½ teaspoon baking soda

¼ teaspoon salt

¼ cup nonfat milk

3 tablespoons canola oil

2 tablespoons nonfat plain Greek yogurt

2 large egg whites, at room temperature

2 teaspoons pure vanilla extract

1 teaspoon grated lemon zest

1 tablespoon freshly squeezed lemon juice

1 tablespoon poppy seeds

1 cup fresh raspberries, rinsed and dried well, each halved

Preheat the oven to 400°F. Line a 12-cup muffin pan with paper liners.

In a bowl, combine the flour, sugar, baking powder, baking soda, and salt.

In a separate bowl, combine the milk, oil, yogurt, egg whites, vanilla extract, and lemon zest and juice.

Add the wet ingredients to the dry and stir until just combined. Stir in the poppy seeds. Carefully fold in the raspberries.

Evenly divide the batter among the 12 muffin cups, filling each about four-fifths full. Bake for 20 to 25 minutes, until a toothpick inserted into the center of a muffin comes out clean. Remove to a cooling rack and allow to cool.

Roasted Eggplant Dip

YIELD: **2 cups, serving 4**

Roasting eggplant infuses it with a smoky-sweet taste that, when blended with garbanzo beans, garlic, and a mix of sesame and cumin seeds, produces a richly flavored dip. Rather than using oil for flavor, I turn to low-sodium vegetable broth for delicious results. Serve the dip with fresh garden veggies.

1 large eggplant, peeled and cut into 1-inch cubes

1 teaspoon olive oil

½ cup low-sodium canned garbanzo beans, drained

¼ cup fresh flat-leaf parsley

2 tablespoons sesame seeds

1 teaspoon whole cumin seeds

1 clove garlic, peeled

3 tablespoons low-sodium vegetable broth

1 tablespoon lemon juice

Preheat the oven to 400°F. Line a baking sheet with aluminum foil.

Place the eggplant on the baking sheet and drizzle with a light coating of olive oil. Season with salt and pepper and toss to evenly distribute. Bake for about 40 minutes, flipping the cubes halfway through, until the eggplant is tender and browned. Remove and allow to cool slightly.

In a food processor, combine the roasted eggplant with 1 teaspoon olive oil, the garbanzo beans, parsley, sesame seeds, cumin seeds, garlic, broth, and lemon juice. Pulse 2 to 3 minutes, until smooth. Season to taste with salt and pepper.

South-of-the-Border Salsa

YIELD: **4 servings**

This is one of my favorite things to snack on, whether I'm at a party with friends or doing my homework. The mix of fresh cilantro and lime juice gives it zing, while the cumin warms every scoopful. Of course, it's perfect with whole grain chips, but it also makes an excellent topping for burgers, chicken, and fish. If you feel like turning up the heat, just toss in a few more chile peppers.

6 medium roma tomatoes, seeded*
and diced

½ cup coarsely chopped fresh
cilantro

½ medium red onion, diced

½ serrano chile pepper, seeded
and diced

1 teaspoon minced garlic

2 teaspoons whole cumin seeds

½ teaspoon coarse salt

1 teaspoon lime juice

Toasted whole wheat pita chips,
for serving (optional)

Combine the tomatoes, cilantro, onion, chile pepper, garlic, cumin, and salt in a large bowl. Add the lime juice and stir gently until thoroughly combined. Serve with pita chips, if desired.

*TIP: Removing the seeds from the tomatoes yields a thicker, chunkier salsa.

Flavored Popcorn, 3 Ways

YIELD: **3 to 4 servings (1½ to 2 cups per serving)**

Popcorn is one of the healthiest, crunchiest snack options around, provided it isn't doused in heavy toppings like melted butter. Pop a batch to take on a road trip or the bus, or for after-school munching. These are three of my favorite versions, but you can use your imagination to come up with even more varieties.

3 tablespoons popcorn kernels

Place the kernels in a brown paper bag. Fold and seal the bag with tape, leaving generous space inside. Microwave on high 1 minute and 30 seconds, or until the kernels are mostly popped but not burnt. Remove the popcorn to a bowl.

Popcorn Italiano

2 tablespoons olive oil

2 tablespoons grated Parmesan cheese

1 tablespoon dried basil

1 tablespoon dried oregano

1 tablespoon garlic powder

¼ teaspoon sea salt

⅛ teaspoon crushed red-pepper flakes

⅛ teaspoon ground black pepper

In a separate bowl, combine the oil, Parmesan, basil, oregano, garlic powder, salt, red-pepper flakes, and black pepper and mix into a thick paste. Add to the popcorn and toss until fully coated.

Wasabi-Chili Popcorn

½ cup wasabi-coated peas

¼ cup pretzel sticks, broken into large pieces

1 teaspoon chili powder

½ teaspoon mustard powder

¼ teaspoon sea salt

Add the wasabi peas and pretzels to the popcorn and toss to combine. In a separate bowl, combine the chili powder, mustard powder, and salt. Sprinkle over the popcorn mixture and toss to ensure all the ingredients are evenly distributed.

Honey-Roasted-Peanut Popcorn

3 tablespoons honey

2 teaspoons ground cinnamon

1 teaspoon pure vanilla extract*

2 cups unsalted raw peanuts

Preheat the oven to 350°F. Line a baking sheet with parchment paper and lightly coat the paper with canola oil.

Microwave the honey in a small microwave-proof bowl on high for about 20 seconds. Stir in the cinnamon and vanilla extract. Toss with the peanuts in a medium bowl until well coated.

Spread the peanuts on the prepared sheet and bake for 5 minutes. Remove, stir to break up any clumps, and bake 5 minutes more, until deep golden. Cool, stirring frequently, for about 5 minutes.

Add the peanuts to the popcorn and gently toss. Mix until evenly distributed without breaking up the popcorn.

*TIP: As an alternative to vanilla extract, try ½ teaspoon ground dried vanilla beans. (The black specks in your favorite vanilla ice cream are vanilla beans.) Check out your local gourmet food shop to find these powdered beans.

Honey-Mustard Dip

YIELD: Scant ½ cup, serving 4

Just two ingredients—mustard and honey—are all it takes to whip up a sweet and tangy-hot dip! It's perfect for drizzling atop a mix of greens or served with cut vegetables.

¼ cup Dijon mustard	2 tablespoons honey

Using a whisk, mix together the mustard and honey until thoroughly incorporated and smooth.

Ranch Dip

YIELD: ¾ cup, serving 4

This creamy, whipped dip is not only lighter and fresher than those made from standard seasoning packets, but it contains far less salt. Set a big bowl in the center of a pile of whole grain chips or a variety of chopped vegetables. (See photo on page 81.)

½ cup light mayonnaise	1 teaspoon minced sweet onion
¼ cup nonfat Greek yogurt	½ teaspoon minced garlic
1 teaspoon minced fresh chives	¼ teaspoon sea salt
1 teaspoon minced fresh flat-leaf parsley	¼ teaspoon ground black pepper
1 teaspoon minced fresh dill	

Mix together the mayonnaise, yogurt, chives, parsley, dill, onion, garlic, salt, and pepper until smooth. Spoon into a bowl and serve.

Banana Split Smoothie

YIELD: **2 servings**

Who doesn't crave a banana split from time to time—or many times, for that matter? In this frosty smoothie, expect all of the indulgence of an authentic banana split, swirled together in a rich and thick drink. Bananas—check! Chocolate—check! Strawberries—check!

1 banana, peeled and frozen

½ cup frozen strawberries

1 cup unsweetened almond milk

2 tablespoons honey

1 tablespoon unsweetened cocoa powder

1 teaspoon pure vanilla extract

Blend the banana, strawberries, milk, honey, cocoa powder, and vanilla extract in a blender until smooth.

Pour the smoothie into 2 serving glasses. Enjoy!

Strawberry-Coconut Chiller

YIELD: **2 servings**

I'm always amazed by the simplicity and deliciousness of this tropical concoction. With just four ingredients, it couldn't be easier to whip up, which I recommend when you need to beat the heat.

1½ cups frozen unsweetened strawberries

¾ cup water

3 tablespoons light agave nectar

1 teaspoon coconut extract

In a blender, puree the strawberries, water, agave nectar, and coconut extract until smooth and evenly distributed.

Pour the smoothie into 2 serving glasses. Enjoy!

Spiced Chai Latte

YIELD: **2 servings**

If you've never enjoyed a sip of traditional chai tea, now you can. Think of your favorite, warm pumpkin pie spices infused into white tea and blended with milk and honey. *Masala chai,* as it is known in India, is widely replicated by many of our favorite coffeehouses, but they frequently begin with a shot of sugary syrup. When you make it at home, you can control the sweetness.

3 cups water

1 tablespoon fennel seeds

15 whole cloves

14 whole allspice

9 whole green cardamom pods

2 pink peppercorns

1 teaspoon finely grated fresh ginger

4 cinnamon sticks

2 bags unflavored decaffeinated white tea

½ cup nonfat milk

Honey or other sweetener (optional)

Foamed nonfat milk,* for garnish

Bring the water to a simmer in a medium saucepan over medium heat.

Meanwhile, place the fennel seeds, cloves, allspice, cardamom, and peppercorns in a mortar and lightly crush with a pestle.** Add to the simmering water, along with the ginger and cinnamon sticks. Stir, cover, and simmer for 20 minutes.

Break open the tea bags and stir the tea leaves into the simmering liquid. Reduce the heat to low and simmer 3 to 4 minutes.

Stir in the milk. Strain the tea through a fine-mesh strainer; discard the cooked spices. Transfer the tea to a large teapot or heatproof pitcher, or evenly divide between 2 mugs. To serve, add honey or other sweetener to taste (if desired) and garnish with foamed milk.

*TIP: To make the creamy, frothy, whipped foam milk available in your favorite coffeehouses, vigorously whisk chilled—or better yet, slightly warmed—milk until the liquid morphs into a fluffy, airy topping. You can also take advantage of special electric milk-frothing "wands" that are inserted into a cup of milk and whisk it up from the inside—a great helping hand for the arms!

**TIP: If you don't have a mortar and pestle, place the seasonings between several layers of paper towels and carefully crush them using a kitchen mallet.

Holiday Peppermint Hot Cocoa

YIELD: **4 servings**

Warm up on a cold winter's night with this silky, sweet drink. The underlying key to this recipe is the combination of bold dark chocolate, fruity vanilla bean, and cool, clean peppermint.

2 cups nonfat milk

2 cups water

½ cup dark chocolate chips

⅓ cup light agave nectar

1 whole vanilla bean, split lengthwise, seeds scraped out and reserved along with the pod

½ teaspoon peppermint extract

Foamed nonfat milk, for garnish (optional) (see the tip on page 173)

Coarsely crushed peppermint candies, for garnish (optional)

Dark chocolate shavings, for garnish (optional)

In a saucepan over medium-high heat, combine the milk, water, chocolate chips, agave nectar, and vanilla bean pod and seeds. Cook, whisking frequently, until the chips are melted and the mixture is smooth, about 5 minutes. Stir in the peppermint extract.

Remove the vanilla pod and divide the cocoa evenly among 4 mugs or coffee cups. Garnish with foamed milk, crushed peppermint candies, and chocolate shavings (as desired).

Chapter 7
Desserts

WE CAMPAIGN TO EAT IT BEFORE DINNER IS SERVED. We lobby for overly generous helpings or seconds—even thirds. There are a million examples of foods that fall into the category we all love and know as dessert.

I am a huge fan of dessert, and I don't think it should be skipped. And after all of my research and recipe developing, I've come to realize that dessert doesn't have to be a guilt-ridden affair that ends up in regret.

For me, finding the balance between indulging and overindulging is the key to having your cake and eating it, too! And for me, that was long a challenge as a sweet tooth runs in my family. It dates back to my parents' childhoods. My mother moved onto the same street as my father when they were both 5 years old. Dad, his sister, and mother (Grandma!) delivered a homemade cake by way of a sled, pulling it through sleet and snow, to welcome my mom's family to the neighborhood. That cake has remained a symbol of the sweet bond between my parents' families; and to me, that's worth keeping up a sweet tooth for!

So, here's the thing: There's no reason to deprive yourself. When you do, it can actually be counterproductive. Trying to avoid sweets only builds temptation and ends in overindulging. Believe me, I've learned this lesson the hard way! But I've devised a plan that has worked for me and, by passing it on, I hope it inspires you, too.

CONTROL YOUR PORTIONS. All of the recipes that follow (and come before these, in fact) include a yield, which lets you know how many servings they make. Get to know these serving sizes, so that when you're out and about and the bakery, ice cream shop, or dessert menu beckons, you'll have a good sense of what constitutes a reasonable portion. Most of the time, any dessert you order in those places will be oversized (or will feature ingredients that aren't readily identifiable). Since dessert is not the most highly nutritious part of a meal, enjoying it in moderation—and savoring every bite—will never lead to regret. One scoop of ice cream has all of the creamy, rich flavor and texture as two or three—and you'll be satisfied . . . I promise!

WORK IN THE NUTRITION. When you think about food that's good for you, dessert likely doesn't come to mind. But carrots, ginger, and blueberries do, right? The truth is you don't have to compromise the lusciousness of a favorite dessert if you add healthful ingredients to the mix. I've managed to work fiber into many recipes in this chapter by swapping out some white flour, which is bleached and stripped of many of its nutrients, for whole wheat flour, whole wheat pastry flour, or oat flour.

TRIM THE FAT. Dessert is almost synonymous with butter, the delicious spread that tastes so irresistibly good swabbed on toast, melted into a baked potato, or whipped into a cake. Unfortunately, it's high in saturated fat (the bad kind) so it's important to limit how much butter you eat—and make the most of the amount you do. I've found that when it comes to butter in desserts, you don't always need as much as you might imagine. I've learned how to cut down on butter by replacing some of it with unsweetened applesauce or heart-healthy, velvety-smooth canola oil. Not only is the result equally as moist and tender as what you would expect from the bakery, but it's lighter, too.

The kewlified desserts you'll find in this chapter—Apple Pot Pies (page 188), Chai Poached Pears (page 196), Peanut Butter–Chocolate Chip Bars (page 192), Oatmeal Raisin Cookies (page 191), and Carrot Cupcakes (page 187), to name a few—will satisfy even the sweetest sweet tooth!

Vanilla-Bean Pound Cake

YIELD: **10 servings**

Vanilla beans, the source of pure vanilla extract, lend not only an intense vanilla flavor to this pound cake, but also their signature black specks—the telltale sign that fresh beans have been used. As for pound cake, it's named for the amount of butter, sugar, and so on that is traditionally used in the recipe—1 pound each! Of course, that's not the case here. My moist version uses nutritious oat flour and a mixture of canola oil and unsweetened applesauce instead, guaranteeing bakery-worthy texture. Wrap up a warm, fresh loaf in parchment for a fantastic gift to share with friends or family . . . or just yourself!

2 cups oat flour

1⅓ cups raw sugar

1 teaspoon baking powder

½ teaspoon sea salt

8 large egg whites

½ cup plus 2 teaspoons unsweetened applesauce

¼ cup canola oil, plus more for the pan

1½ teaspoons pure vanilla extract

Seeds scraped from 1 vanilla bean

Preheat the oven to 350°F. Coat an 8- by 4-inch loaf pan with canola oil.

In a large mixing bowl, combine the flour, sugar, baking powder, and salt. In a separate bowl, combine the egg whites, applesauce, oil, vanilla extract, and vanilla seeds. Gradually incorporate the wet ingredients into the dry and stir until just combined.

Pour the batter into the prepared loaf pan. Bake for 40 minutes, or until a toothpick inserted into the center of the cake comes out clean. Cool for at least 10 minutes, then invert onto a dish or cooling rack. Cut into 10 slices to serve.

Mini Chocolate Lava Cakes

YIELD: **6 servings**

Dark chocolate—specifically, the 70-percent-or-more-cacao variety—is robust in flavor, so a little goes a long way. Plus, it's jam-packed with antioxidants. These little cakes are so rich that just a few bites will satisfy—and that's the key.

6 teaspoons plus 4 tablespoons fine granulated (caster) sugar, divided

½ cup unsweetened natural cocoa powder, plus more for dusting

¼ cup plus 2 tablespoons hot water

1 tablespoon unsalted butter

3 tablespoons whole wheat pastry flour

3 tablespoons light agave nectar

9 tablespoons dark chocolate chips, divided

2 teaspoons pure vanilla extract

¾ cup nonfat milk

4 large egg whites

Preheat the oven to 350°F. Lightly coat six 7- or 8-ounce ramekins with canola oil. Fill each with 1 teaspoon fine sugar, rotating the ramekin until the sugar has evenly coated the bottom and sides. Discard excess sugar.

In a large mixing bowl, combine the cocoa powder and hot water.

In a medium saucepan, melt the butter over medium heat. Stir in 1 tablespoon of the sugar, the flour, agave nectar, 3 tablespoons of the chocolate chips, and vanilla extract. Cook 1 to 2 minutes. Slowly pour in the milk, whisking constantly, and gently simmer until the mixture begins to thicken, 3 to 4 minutes. Stir into the large bowl with the cocoa mixture.

In a separate, large, very clean mixing bowl, beat the egg whites with an electric hand mixer on medium to high speed until frothy. Gradually add the remaining 3 tablespoons sugar, 1 tablespoon at a time, until the whites are glossy and feature stiff peaks.

Gently fold one-fourth of the egg whites at a time into the chocolate mixture using a large spatula, until no streaks remain and being careful not to deflate or overbeat the mixture.

Spoon the mixture into the prepared ramekins, filling each halfway. Coarsely chop the remaining 6 tablespoons chocolate chips. Add 1 tablespoon to the center of the batter in each ramekin. Top with the remaining batter until the ramekins are filled nearly to the top.

Place the ramekins on a baking sheet and bake 15 to 18 minutes, until the soufflés have risen and tremble slightly when the baking sheet is gently shaken, dust with cocoa powder. Serve immediately.

Lemon-Almond Angel Food Cake with Vanilla Bean

YIELD: **8 to 10 servings**

The delicious combination of lemon and almond whisks me right back to Sorrento, a picturesque seaside village in southern Italy that overlooks the azure waves of the Mediterranean. Angel food cake is remarkable for its cloud-like texture. Mostly composed of egg whites, angel food cake is super-low in fat and one of the healthier options when it comes to dessert. Keep its sugar content in mind, though—and, most importantly, remember that just a sliver will satisfy your sweet tooth. Serve it with a colorful mix of fresh berries.

1½ cups confectioners' sugar

1 cup cake flour

12 large egg whites, at room temperature

1½ teaspoons cream of tartar

½ teaspoon freshly squeezed lemon juice

1 cup fine granulated (caster) sugar

1½ teaspoons freshly grated lemon zest

1¼ teaspoons almond extract

Seeds scraped from 2 vanilla beans

Preheat the oven to 350°F. Using a fine-mesh strainer, sift the confectioners' sugar and flour together into a medium bowl. Set aside.

In the bowl of an electric stand mixer fitted with the whisk attachment (or with a hand mixer), beat the egg whites on medium speed until foamy. Add the cream of tartar and lemon juice, raise the speed to medium high, and beat until the egg whites are at the soft-peak stage.*

Mixing constantly, gradually incorporate the fine sugar into the egg whites, 1 tablespoon at a time, until the mixture is glossy and the whites are at the stiff-peak stage.* Add the lemon zest, almond extract, and vanilla seeds. Mix until evenly distributed.

Resift about one-quarter of the sugar-flour mixture over the egg whites, then fold it in with a large, flexible spatula until no streaks remain; be careful not to deflate the egg whites. Repeat with the remaining sugar mixture, incorporating one-quarter at a time.

Transfer the batter to a large, ungreased angel food cake or tube pan with a removable base and smooth the top. Bake for 40 to 45 minutes, until a toothpick inserted into the cake comes out clean.

With the cake still in the pan, invert the central tube of the pan onto a tall, narrow, empty bottle, or perch the pan, upside down, onto several cans positioned at the pan's edges. Allow to cool completely. Cut around the edges of the cake with a paring knife and remove the base of the pan, then cut around the base to release the cake onto a serving plate.

*TIP: When it comes to whipping egg whites, here's what *soft peaks* and *stiff peaks* mean: When you quickly pull the whisk or beater out of the eggs, they should form *soft peaks* that fall to the side slightly. In contrast, *stiff peaks* will hold their shape and stay firm and upright.

Carrot Cupcakes

YIELD: **12 cupcakes**

Nonfat yogurt and canola oil replace butter in these classic cupcakes, which I dip in a simple icing made from powdered sugar and low-fat milk. Yum!

FOR THE CUPCAKES

1 cup all-purpose flour

½ cup whole wheat pastry flour

1 teaspoon baking powder

½ teaspoon baking soda

1 teaspoon ground cinnamon

¼ teaspoon ground allspice

½ teaspoon sea salt

¾ cup canola oil

2 tablespoons nonfat plain yogurt

¾ cup raw sugar

2 large eggs

1 teaspoon pure vanilla extract

1½ cups finely grated carrots

¼ cup golden raisins

FOR THE ICING

1½ cups confectioners' sugar

7½ tablespoons nonfat milk

2 teaspoons unsalted butter, melted

½ teaspoon pure vanilla extract

Preheat the oven to 375°F. Line a 12-cup muffin pan with paper liners.

In a medium bowl, whisk together the all-purpose flour, whole wheat flour, baking powder, baking soda, cinnamon, allspice, and salt. In the bowl of a standing mixer fitted with the paddle attachment, beat the oil, yogurt, and raw sugar on medium speed. Add the eggs, one at a time, mixing constantly. Mix in the vanilla extract. Reduce the speed, and add the dry ingredients in 3 portions, mixing until incorporated before adding the next. Stir in the carrots and raisins.

Fill each muffin cup about three-fourths full with the batter. Bake for 20 to 25 minutes, or until a toothpick inserted into the center comes out clean. Remove to a rack to cool completely.

To make the icing, place the confectioners' sugar in a medium bowl. In a separate bowl, combine the milk, butter, and vanilla extract. Pour into the sugar, mixing constantly with a fork or spoon, until the icing is smooth, thick, and glossy. Dip the top of each cupcake into the icing and swirl to cover in a thick, even layer.

TIP: Garnish the iced cupcakes with edible 24-karat gold leaf for a ritzy-glitzy topping—a reasonable, yet completely optional, splurge! It can be found online or at baking supply stores.

Apple Pot Pies

YIELD: **6 servings**

I love apple pie (who doesn't?), but not the version with a butter-laden double crust. My flaky, crumbly honey-oat streusel, which is made without any butter, tops off fragrant spiced apples. By baking these in individual ramekins, you're already taking a great first step toward portion control.

FOR THE CRUSTS

3 (9-inch) store-bought unbaked pie crusts

1 large egg white, lightly beaten

FOR THE FILLING

1½ cups unsweetened applesauce

¾ cup raw sugar

1 tablespoon ground cinnamon

1 teaspoon ground allspice

½ teaspoon ground cloves

½ teaspoon freshly grated or ground nutmeg

¼ teaspoon sea salt

6 large sweet red apples, peeled, cored, and cut into ½-inch wedges (about 8 cups)

1 tablespoon all-purpose flour

1 tablespoon whole wheat pastry flour

FOR THE STREUSEL TOPPING

1½ cups instant oats

1 cup plus 2 tablespoons all-purpose flour

¼ cup plus 2 tablespoons whole wheat pastry flour

¾ cup packed light brown sugar

1½ teaspoons ground cinnamon

¼ cup plus 2 tablespoons canola oil

¼ cup plus 2 tablespoons honey

Preheat the oven to 350°F. Lightly coat six 7-ounce ovenproof ramekins and a large baking sheet (or 6 individual baking dishes) with canola oil.

For the crusts, fit enough pie crust dough into each ramekin so that about ½ inch of dough hangs over the edges. (Fit the dough into the ramekins well, so that the dough takes on the shape of the ramekin.) Use kitchen shears to trim the edges. Using the tines of a fork, crimp the edge of the dough where it meets the top of the ramekin.* Lightly brush the pie crust with the egg white. Set aside.

(continued)

*TIP: Crimping is a great way to ensure that the dough holds onto the ramekin. It simply means pressing gently into the dough with the tines of a fork to make light indentations.

For the filling, in a medium saucepan, whisk to combine the applesauce, raw sugar, cinnamon, allspice, cloves, nutmeg, and salt. Cook over medium heat, whisking often, for 20 minutes, or until the sugar has dissolved into the applesauce and the liquid is thick and very fragrant. The texture of the sauce for the filling should resemble a cross between gooey caramel and rich peanut butter. Let cool, whisking frequently, for 5 minutes.

Place the apple wedges in a large heatproof mixing bowl. Pour the warm sauce over and toss with a heatproof spatula or spoon. Stir in the all-purpose and whole wheat flours until evenly distributed.

Distribute the apple mixture equally among the 6 dough-lined ramekins. Use the back of a spoon to lightly pack down the mixture.

For the streusel, in a medium bowl, thoroughly combine the oats, all-purpose flour, whole wheat flour, brown sugar, and cinnamon. Add the oil and honey and work the mixture with your fingers until it becomes pliable enough to squeeze into a tight ball. Use your fingertips to break the ball into randomly sized chunks.

Place the filled ramekins on the baking sheet (or in the individual baking dishes). Top each with the streusel, ensuring a significant layer of streusel for each. Lightly press the streusel onto the filling, but do not pack the crumbs together. If any streusel falls onto the baking sheet or dishes, place it atop a pie again. Bake for 1 hour 10 minutes, or until the streusel topping and exposed crust are golden brown.*

Let cool for at least 10 minutes before serving. (WARNING: Ramekins still might be hot!)

*TIP: If any of the juices run over the sides during baking, don't worry; the canola oil will prevent the ramekins from sticking to the bottom of the baking sheet or dishes.

Oatmeal Raisin Cookies

YIELD: **24 cookies**

Crispy on the outside, chewy on the inside, this revamped version of the classic makes use of unsweetened applesauce to keep the cookies moist and whole wheat pastry flour to give them a deeper, more toothsome texture.

¾ cup all-purpose flour

¼ cup whole wheat pastry flour

1 teaspoon ground cinnamon

1 teaspoon baking powder

½ teaspoon baking soda

¼ teaspoon sea salt

2 tablespoons unsalted butter, at room temperature

⅔ cup raw sugar

1 large egg, at room temperature

¼ cup unsweetened applesauce

2 teaspoons pure vanilla extract

1½ cups instant oats

¾ cup raisins

Preheat the oven to 350°F. Line 2 large baking sheets with parchment paper.

In a bowl, combine the all-purpose flour, whole wheat flour, cinnamon, baking powder, baking soda, and salt.

In the bowl of an electric stand mixer fitted with the paddle attachment (or using a hand mixer), cream the butter and sugar on medium speed. Add the egg, applesauce, and vanilla extract and mix until smooth. Gradually incorporate the dry ingredients, mixing constantly, until just combined. Stir in the oats and raisins.

Drop 24 rounded tablespoons of batter onto the baking sheets, spacing them about 2 inches apart. Bake on the center rack, one baking sheet at a time if necessary, for 12 to 15 minutes, until golden brown. Remove the cookies to wire racks and allow to cool completely.

Peanut Butter–Chocolate Chip Bars

YIELD: **16 bars**

In elementary school, one of my all-time favorite afternoon snacks was a flaky, cakey chocolate chip cookie. In an effort to create a healthier version, I replaced some of the white flour with whole wheat flour and substituted peanut butter for some of the butter. Intensify the flavor of rich dark chocolate by stirring a little bit of espresso powder into the mix.

¾ cup all-purpose flour

½ cup whole wheat pastry flour

1½ teaspoons baking powder

1 teaspoon espresso powder

¼ teaspoon sea salt

1 cup raw sugar

¼ cup unsalted butter

¼ cup creamy peanut butter

2 teaspoons pure vanilla extract

1 large egg

1 large egg white

½ cup dark chocolate chips

½ cup peanut butter chips

Preheat the oven to 350°F. Lightly coat a 10-inch square baking pan with canola oil.

In a mixing bowl, combine the all-purpose flour, whole wheat flour, baking powder, espresso powder, and salt.

In the bowl of a standing mixer fitted with the paddle attachment (or using a hand mixer), beat the sugar, butter, peanut butter, and vanilla extract for about 1 minute, until smooth. Add the egg and egg white and beat 1 minute on medium speed. Gradually incorporate the flour mixture, mixing constantly. Stir in the chocolate and peanut butter chips.

Spread the batter in the pan and bake for about 35 minutes, or until the bars are golden brown and a toothpick inserted into the center comes out clean. Transfer to a wire rack and allow to cool completely before slicing into 16 squares.

Blueberry Crumble

YIELD: **6 servings**

Keep it simple and rustic—that's the best way to go when fresh, juicy berries are at their peak. I use blueberries (they're loaded with antioxidants, and the more of those you take in, the better), but any other berry or pitted stone fruit works just as well here.

FOR THE STREUSEL TOPPING

1½ cups instant oats

1 cup plus 2 tablespoons all-purpose flour

¼ cup plus 2 tablespoons whole wheat pastry flour

¾ cup packed light brown sugar

1½ teaspoons ground cinnamon

¼ cup plus 2 tablespoons canola oil

¼ cup plus 2 tablespoons honey

FOR THE FILLING

2 tablespoons freshly squeezed orange juice

2 teaspoons pure vanilla extract

1 tablespoon cornstarch

4 cups blueberries

⅓ cup raw sugar

1 tablespoon whole wheat pastry flour

¼ teaspoon sea salt

Preheat the oven to 350°F. Line a baking sheet with parchment paper. Lightly coat six 8-ounce round ramekins with canola oil.

For the streusel, in a medium bowl thoroughly combine the oats, all-purpose flour, whole wheat flour, brown sugar, and cinnamon. Add the oil and honey and work the mixture with your fingers until it becomes pliable enough to squeeze into a tight ball. Break the ball into randomly sized chunks.

For the filling, in a large bowl, combine the orange juice, vanilla extract, and cornstarch and mix until smooth. Add the blueberries, raw sugar, flour, and salt and toss to combine.

Divide the blueberry filling among the ramekins. Top each with a thick layer of streusel.

Place the ramekins on the baking sheet and bake for 50 minutes, until the topping is golden brown. Let cool at least 10 minutes before serving. Serve warm or allow to cool completely.

Chai Poached Pears

YIELD: **6 servings**

Inspired by the desserts I've enjoyed in some of Paris's extraordinary bistros, brasseries, and patisseries, these poached pears are far simpler to make than they look. Saffron imbues the sauce with its unique amber hue, and cinnamon, allspice, and cloves infuse it with the exotic flavors of Indian chai.

8 cinnamon sticks

1 tablespoon whole allspice

2 teaspoons whole cloves

4 cups water

3 cups unsweetened apple juice

1 tablespoon freshly grated orange zest

1 cup freshly squeezed orange juice

½ teaspoon saffron threads

6 Bosc pears, peeled, stems left on

In cheesecloth or a paper tea filter, combine the cinnamon sticks, allspice, and cloves. Seal and tie tightly with kitchen twine.

In a large saucepan or Dutch oven, combine the spice packet, water, apple juice, orange zest and juice, and saffron. Cover and bring to a boil over high heat. Reduce the heat and add the pears. Cover and simmer for 30 to 35 minutes, until the pears are fork-tender. Remove the pears to a plate. Continue to boil the sauce over high heat, uncovered, until reduced and thickened slightly, about 15 minutes. Discard the packet of spices.

Place 1 pear on each of 6 serving plates. Divide the sauce evenly among each serving, drizzling it over the pears.

Lemon-Lime Kewlers

YIELD: **16 kewlers**

These delicious, refreshing "kewlers" are the perfect way to bring down the temperature on a hot summer day. While many coolers are loaded with sugar, I rely on agave nectar, an all-natural liquid sweetener that's similar to honey in viscosity, but less assertive in flavor. The waiting game begins once you put the mixture in the freezer, but the fun starts when you scrape it up with a fork into an airy Italian ice. I like to keep a backup batch of this on hand in the freezer—it'll revitalize you when the mercury starts to rise!

1 cup light agave nectar

3½ cups boiling water

¼ cup plus 2 tablespoons lemon juice

¼ cup plus 2 tablespoons lime juice

8 lemons

8 limes

16 small mint leaves, for garnish

In a large heatproof and freezer-proof bowl, whisk the agave nectar into the hot water until it has completely dissolved. Add the lemon and lime juices and whisk until incorporated. Freeze for at least 8 hours or overnight.

Slice a small portion off the bottom of each lemon and lime so that they can stand vertically on their own. Slice a larger portion off the tops and hollow out with a melon baller until no flesh remains inside the fruit. Set aside.

Once the lemon-lime mixture is frozen, remove from the freezer and scrape it repeatedly with a spoon or the tines of a fork until the result is light, fluffy ice.

Spoon the icy lemon-lime mixture into the lemons and limes and garnish with mint leaves. Serve immediately, while they're chilly!

Watermelon-Lime Ice Pops

YIELD: **12 to 15 ice pops**

Nothing says summer like a frozen ice pop. The upside of making your own is that you can concoct all kinds of unique flavor combinations. I love the fusion of watermelon and lime—mixed with a little bit of agave nectar, summer doesn't get any sweeter.

> **6 cups watermelon chunks**
>
> **½ cup light agave nectar**
>
> **¼ cup plus 2 tablespoons lime juice**
>
> **¼ teaspoon pure vanilla extract**

Blend the watermelon chunks, agave nectar, lime juice, and vanilla extract in a blender until smooth. Strain into a pitcher.

Pour the liquid into ice pop molds and transfer to the freezer. Freeze for about 1 hour, until the ice pops are stiff enough to hold sticks, but not yet completely frozen. Insert ice pop sticks into each mold (or insert sticks according to manufacturer's instructions) and return to the freezer and freeze until solid.

THE KEWLBITES™ PANTRY

SWEETENERS AND OILS

Honey

Agave nectar

Maple syrup

Raw sugar*

Olive oil

Canola oil

CANNED GOODS

Low-sodium canned beans:
white (cannellini),
red kidney, black

Canned vegetables: hearts
of palm, artichoke hearts,
whole/peeled and crushed
tomatoes

Low-sodium chicken broth

Unsweetened cocoa powder

Peanut butter

WHOLE GRAINS
AND PASTA

Farro

Quinoa

Instant oats

Steel-cut oats

Whole grain brown rice

Whole wheat panko bread crumbs

Whole wheat flour

Whole wheat pastry flour

Wheat germ

100 percent whole wheat
pasta

100 percent whole wheat
wraps

SEASONINGS,
BAKING INGREDIENTS,
AND MORE

Sea salt**

Reduced-sodium soy sauce

Dried herbs and spices: basil,
dill, mustard powder, chili
powder, onion powder,
garlic powder, cinnamon,
allspice

Pure vanilla extract

Baking powder

Baking soda

Dark chocolate: bars, chips . . .
any form, but keep it dark

Dried fruits: apricots,
cranberries, blueberries,
raisins, etc.

Raw nuts: pecans, walnuts,
almonds, peanuts,
pistachios, cashews

White tuna (packed in water)

Popcorn kernels

Unsweetened applesauce

*RAW SUGAR: Throughout the recipes here, I often make use of raw sugar—sometimes called "natural cane sugar" or "turbinado sugar"—as opposed to regular white table sugar. The latter is bleached and stripped of any trace nutrients present within the sugar cane, while the former is a more natural, wholesome choice. While it's calorically equivalent to regular sugar, it's a step in the right direction and has a crystalline texture and amber color, distinguishing it from its typical white counterpart. You can find it shelved alongside regular sugar. It sweetens, dissolves, and cooks up just like ordinary sugar, but it's a better choice.

**SEA SALT: Sea salt, as its apropos name suggests, is sourced from the sea. The process of harvesting it involves allowing the water to evaporate, leaving behind the salt along with trace minerals that can lend it unique tastes or hues. Besides the natural origins of sea salt, there are other benefits to keeping a jar in your pantry. First: It's inexpensive and you can find it in just about every supermarket (hooray!). Second: It doesn't contain any additives or anti-caking agents like table salt does. Third: While there are varying textures and types of sea salt (coarse, fine, and others), many types' rough textures make this salt a great choice for sprinkling onto or garnishing certain foods for a final flourish before serving. While there are a multitude of sea salts available today—some even come in vivid colors, like pink, black, or green (!)— for everyday cooking and the recipes that call for salt in this book, I recommend keeping a bottle of standard fine-grained sea salt on hand.

Acknowledgments

Big thanks go to my family—especially my mother, Michelle, who has been my biggest supporter, confidante, and best friend throughout my life and career. I'm so fortunate to have in you an incredible source of wisdom, knowledge, and fortitude. Thank-you, mom, for the huge sacrifices of time, energy, and hard work you've made on my behalf. You are a trooper—making endless trips to the supermarket, doing rounds of dirty dishes, trekking through airport after airport, and handling 100 recipe-tasting sessions with grace and patience. Thanks are also in order to my father, Adam, and my grandparents, Caryn and Michael. They have all cheered me on every step of the way.

I am so very grateful to the extraordinary and brilliant team of professionals and mentors who have helped me realize my dreams and ambitions. Foremost among them is my spectacular literary agent, Michael Psaltis. I also owe a great deal of appreciation to my ingenious editor Kathleen Hackett, art director Amy King, photographer Tara Donne, culinary stylist Simon Andrews, and prop stylist Molly FitzSimons for coming together to make a book I am so very proud of. And to the rest of the Rodale team—my deepest gratitude.

Index

Underscored page references indicate boxed text. **Boldfaced** page references indicate photographs.

Conversion Chart

These equivalents have been slightly rounded to make measuring easier.

Volume Measurements

U.S.	IMPERIAL	METRIC
¼ tsp	–	1 ml
½ tsp	–	2 ml
1 tsp	–	5 ml
1 Tbsp	–	15 ml
2 Tbsp (1 oz)	1 fl oz	30 ml
¼ cup (2 oz)	2 fl oz	60 ml
⅓ cup (3 oz)	3 fl oz	80 ml
½ cup (4 oz)	4 fl oz	120 ml
⅔ cup (5 oz)	5 fl oz	160 ml
¾ cup (6 oz)	6 fl oz	180 ml
1 cup (8 oz)	8 fl oz	240 ml

Weight Measurements

U.S.	METRIC
1 oz	30 g
2 oz	60 g
4 oz (¼ lb)	115 g
5 oz (⅓ lb)	145 g
6 oz	170 g
7 oz	200 g
8 oz (½ lb)	230 g
10 oz	285 g
12 oz (¾ lb)	340 g
14 oz	400 g
16 oz (1 lb)	455 g
2.2 lb	1 kg

Length Measurements

U.S.	METRIC
¼"	0.6 cm
½"	1.25 cm
1"	2.5 cm
2"	5 cm
4"	11 cm
6"	15 cm
8"	20 cm
10"	25 cm
12" (1')	30 cm
2.2 lb	1 kg

Pan Sizes

U.S.	METRIC
8" cake pan	20 × 4 cm sandwich or cake tin
9" cake pan	23 × 3.5 cm sandwich or cake tin
11" × 7" baking pan	28 × 18 cm baking tin
13" × 9" baking pan	32.5 × 23 cm baking tin
15" × 10" baking pan	38 × 25.5 cm baking tin
	(Swiss roll tin)
1½ qt baking dish	1.5 liter baking dish
2 qt baking dish	2 liter baking dish
2 qt rectangular baking dish	30 × 19 cm baking dish
9" pie plate	22 × 4 or 23 × 4 cm pie plate
7" or 8" springform pan	18 or 20 cm springform or
	loose-bottom cake tin
9" × 5" loaf pan	23 × 13 cm or 2 lb narrow
	loaf tin or pâté tin

Temperatures

FAHRENHEIT	CENTIGRADE	GAS
140°	60°	–
160°	70°	–
180°	80°	–
225°	105°	¼
250°	120°	½
275°	135°	1
300°	150°	2
325°	160°	3
350°	180°	4
375°	190°	5
400°	200°	6
425°	220°	7
450°	230°	8
475°	245°	9
500°	260°	–